PRAYING THE PSALTER

(WITH OTHERS)

DAVID RAPP

WESTBOW PRESS®
A DIVISION OF THOMAS NELSON & ZONDERVAN

WestBow Press books may be ordered through booksellers or by contacting:

WestBow Press
A Division of Thomas Nelson & Zondervan
1663 Liberty Drive
Bloomington, IN 47403
www.westbowpress.com
844-714-3454

ISBN: 979-8-3850-1478-1 (sc)
ISBN: 979-8-3850-1479-8 (e)

Library of Congress Control Number: 2023924689

Print information available on the last page.

WestBow Press rev. date: 01/09/2025

INTRODUCTION

As I have always heard and known the Psalms to be "songs of prayer" and recognized the prayerful nature of most of them, I found myself wanting to pray them verbatim, only to feel thwarted routinely because the psalmist would change his audience, from man to God, back and forth, frequently within the same Psalm. A good example of this is found in Psalm 23. It begins by talking *about* God, "The Lord is my shepherd." (verse 1) Then, it is directed *to* God, "You are with me." (verse 4). Then, it concludes by again talking *about* God: "And I will dwell in the house of the Lord forever." (verse 6).

This "problem" created in me a desire to adjust the text so that I could pray it, with all of it directed toward God. In doing so, I quickly discovered that I had to be ok with taking some liberties with the text. My goal was to provide seamless prayers that stay as close to the text of the Psalms as possible, using various versions throughout, to create a flow that I am comfortable with and understand. That is to say, my goal was not to rewrite the Psalms but merely to create prayers that I can read and pray, using words and phrases that I would use, while staying as true to the Psalms as possible.

This led me to the next "problem" I encountered, namely that some Psalms seem largely inapplicable to us today. Some are based on the psalmist's unique experiences, as he recalls specific victories over or deliverance from enemies. With some, he calls on God to destroy his adversaries. Some are written specifically to or about Israel or Jerusalem. And some seem to be merely a message or a history lesson to the reader, more than a prayer to God. Accordingly, after much prayer and careful consideration I took some liberties with the text, using my best effort to maintain the heart of the Scripture, to transform all 150 Psalms into prayers, continually directed *to* God, and adding, at the bottom of each, some attributes of God revealed in the Psalm above.

"Messing" with Scripture caused me to really struggle through the process, taking more than seven years to write this. The following quote from historian, Arnold J. Toynbee, however, encouraged me to finish strong and with confidence, knowing that this cannot be perfect and does not have to be:

"All human work is imperfect, because human nature is;
and this intrinsic imperfection of human affairs
cannot be overcome by procrastination."

Though this is surely far from perfect, I hope it blesses you.

1

Lord, please keep us from listening
    to the advice of the wicked.
Keep us from standing in the path of sinners.
Keep us from sitting in the seat of scoffers.

Our delight is in Your law.
Give us the desire and the discipline
    to meditate on it day and night.

We know that, by doing so, we will be like trees
    firmly planted by streams of water,
    which yield their fruit in season and
    whose leaves do not wither;
    And in whatever we do, we will prosper.

You tell us that the wicked are not so,
    that they are like chaff which the wind drives away.
You tell us that the wicked will not stand in the judgment,
    nor will sinners be in the assembly of the righteous.
You tell us that You guard the way of the righteous and
    that the way of the wicked will perish.

Please watch over our paths
    and keep us far from the way of the wicked,
    towards which we are so prone to drift.

You guard our way.

2

Why are the nations so angry?
Why do they waste their time with futile plans?
The kings of the earth prepare for battle,
  and the rulers plot together against You, LORD,
  and against Your anointed.
"Let us break their chains," they cry,
  "and free ourselves from slavery to God."
But You, the One who sits in the heavens, laugh.
You scoff at them.
You speak to them in Your anger and terrify them
  in Your fury, saying:

  "I HAVE INSTALLED MY KING UPON ZION,
    MY HOLY MOUNTAIN."

We will surely tell of Your decree—that Jesus is Your son
  and that You are His father.
You will give Him the nations as His inheritance
  and the whole earth as His possession.
He will break those who oppose Him with a rod of iron
  and dash them to pieces like pottery.
The rulers of the world, therefore, should act wisely
  and take warning.

We will serve You with reverence and rejoice with trembling.
We will submit to Your Son, that He not become angry,
  and we die in the midst of all our activities,
  for His anger can flare up in an instant.
LORD, what a joy it is to take refuge in Your Son.

You are mighty.
You are sovereign.
You are our refuge.

3

O Lord, we have so many enemies; So many are against us.
So many are saying, "God will never rescue them!"
But You, O Lord, are a shield around us;
You are our glory and the lifter of our heads.

We cry out to You,
and You answer from Your holy mountain.
We lay down and slept, and we woke up again, in safety,
for You were watching over us.
We are not afraid of ten thousand enemies
who surround us on every side.

Arise, O Lord! Save us, God!
Slap our enemies in the face!
Shatter the teeth of the wicked!
Salvation comes from You, Lord.
Please bless us.

You are a shield around us.
You are our glory.
You are the lifter of our heads.
You answer us when we cry out to You.
You watch over us.
You save us.

4

Answer us when we call, O God who declares us innocent!
You have freed us from our troubles;
    Have mercy on us and hear our prayer.

No matter how long people try to ruin our reputations,
    make groundless accusations against us,
    or tell lies about us,
We know that You set apart the godly for Yourself.
You hear us when we call.

We will not sin by letting anger control us.
We will meditate in our hearts overnight and remain silent.
We will offer the sacrifices of righteousness and
    trust in You, Lord.

Many people say, "Who will show us better times?"
Let Your face smile on us, Lord.
You have given us greater joy than those
    who have abundant harvests of grain and new wine.
In peace we will lie down and sleep, for You alone, Lord,
    will keep us safe.

You are our liberator.
You hear us when we call.
You give us joy.
You are our protector.

5

O Lord, hear us as we pray;
Pay attention to our groaning.
Listen to our cry for help, our King and our God,
for we pray to no one but You.

In the morning, O Lord, You will hear our voices.
In the morning, we will order our prayers to You
and eagerly watch.
O God, You take no pleasure in wickedness;
You cannot tolerate the sins of the wicked.

Therefore, the proud will not stand in Your presence,
for You hate all who do evil.
You will destroy those who tell lies.
You detest murderers and deceivers.

Because of Your unfailing love, we can enter Your house;
We will worship at Your temple with deepest awe.
Lead us in the right path, O Lord,
or our enemies will conquer us.
Make Your way plain for us to follow.

Our enemies cannot speak a truthful word.
Their deepest desire is to destroy others.
Their talk is foul, like the stench from an open grave.
Their tongues are filled with flattery.

O God, declare them guilty.
Let them be caught in their own traps.
Drive them away because of their many sins,
for they have rebelled against You.

You take no pleasure in wickedness.

But let all who take refuge in You rejoice;
Let them sing joyful praises forever.
Spread Your protection over them, that all
who love Your name may be filled with joy.

For You bless the godly, O LORD;
You surround them with Your shield of love.

You bless the godly.

6

Lord, don't rebuke us in Your anger
 or discipline us in Your rage.
Have mercy on us, Lord, for we are weak.
Heal us, Lord, for our bones are in agony.
Our souls are in deep anguish.
How long, O Lord, until You restore us?

Return, Lord, and rescue us!
Save us because of Your unfailing love.
For the dead do not remember You.
Who can praise You from the grave?

We are exhausted from sobbing;
 All night long we flood our beds with weeping,
 drenching them with our tears.
Our vision is blurred by grief;
 Our eyes are worn out because of all our enemies.

Lord, make all who behave wickedly depart from us.
For You, O Lord, have heard our weeping.
You have heard our appeal for mercy.
You will answer our prayer.
Make all our enemies be humiliated and terrified.
Make them suddenly turn back in shame.

You answer our prayers.

7

We come to You for protection, O LORD our God.
Save us from our persecutors—rescue us!
If You don't, they will maul us like a lion,
  tearing us to pieces with no one to rescue us.
O LORD our God, if we have done wrong
  or are guilty of injustice,
If we have betrayed friends
  or plundered our enemies without cause,
  then let our enemies capture us.
Let them trample us into the ground
  and drag our honor in the dust.

Arise, O LORD, in anger!
Stand up against the fury of our enemies!
Wake up, our God, and bring justice!
Gather the nations before You.
Rule over them from on high.
You judge the nations.
Declare us righteous, O LORD,
For we are innocent, O Most High!
End the evil of those who are wicked,
  and defend the righteous.
For You look deep within the mind and heart,
  O righteous God.

God, You are our shield, saving those
  whose hearts are true and right.
You are an honest judge.
You are angry with the wicked every day.

You judge the nations.
You are our shield.

If a person does not repent, You will sharpen Your sword;
    You will bend and string Your bow.
You will prepare Your deadly weapons
    and shoot Your flaming arrows.

The wicked conceive evil;
    They are pregnant with trouble and give birth to lies.
They dig a deep pit to trap others, then fall into it themselves.
The trouble they make for others backfires on them.
The violence they plan falls on their own heads.

We will thank You, Lord, because You are just;
    We will sing praise to Your name, O Lord Most High.

You are just.

8

O Lord, our Lord, how majestic is Your name
in all the earth!
Your glory is higher than the heavens.
You have taught children and infants to tell of Your strength,
silencing Your enemies and all who oppose You.

When we look at the night sky and see the work of Your
fingers—the moon and the stars You set in place—
what are mere mortals that You should think about them,
human beings that You should care for them?
Yet You made them only a little lower than You
and crowned them with glory and honor.
You gave them charge of everything You made,
putting all things under their authority—
the flocks and the herds
and all the wild animals,
the birds in the sky, the fish in the sea,
and everything that swims the ocean currents.

O Lord, our Lord, how majestic is Your name
in all the earth!

You are majestic.
You created everything.

9

We will praise You, Lord, with all our heart;
We will tell of all the marvelous things You have done.
We will be filled with joy because of You.
We will sing praises to Your name, O Most High.

David's enemies retreated;
They staggered and died when You appeared.
For You judged in his favor; From Your throne,
You judged with fairness.
You rebuked the nations and destroyed the wicked;
You erased their names forever.
The enemy is finished, in endless ruins;
The cities You uprooted are now forgotten.

But You, Lord, reign forever,
executing judgment from Your throne.
You will judge the world with justice
and rule the nations with fairness.
You are a shelter for the oppressed,
a refuge in times of trouble.
Those who know Your name trust in You.
For You do not abandon those who search for You.

We will sing praises to You who reigns in Jerusalem.
We will tell the world about Your unforgettable deeds.
For You who avenge murder also care for the helpless.
You do not ignore the cries of those who suffer.

You reign forever.
You care for the helpless.
You are a shelter for the oppressed.

LORD, have mercy on us.
See how our enemies torment us.
Snatch us back from the jaws of death.
Save us so we can praise You publicly,
so we can rejoice that You have rescued us.

The nations have fallen into the pit they dug for others.
Their own feet have been caught in the trap they set.
You are known for Your justice.
The wicked are trapped by their own deeds.

The wicked will go down to the grave.
This is the fate of all the nations who ignore You.
But the needy will not be ignored forever;
The hopes of the poor will not always be crushed.

Arise, O LORD!
Do not let mere mortals defy You!
Judge the nations! Make them tremble in fear, O LORD.
Let the nations know they are merely human.

You are just.

10

O Lord, why do You stand so far away?
Why do You hide when we are in trouble?
The wicked arrogantly hunt down the poor.
Let them be caught in the evil they plan for others.
For they brag about their evil desires;
They praise the greedy and curse You.

The wicked are too proud to seek You.
They seem to think that You are dead.
Yet they succeed in everything they do.
They do not see Your punishment awaiting them.
They sneer at all their enemies.
They think, "Nothing bad will ever happen to us!
We will be free of trouble forever!"

Their mouths are full of cursing, lies, and threats.
Trouble and evil are on the tips of their tongues.
They lurk in ambush in the villages,
waiting to murder innocent people.
They are always searching for helpless victims.
Like lions crouched in hiding,
they wait to pounce on the helpless.
Like hunters they capture the helpless
and drag them away in nets.
Their helpless victims are crushed;
They fall beneath the strength of the wicked.
The wicked think, "God isn't watching me!
He has closed his eyes and won't even see what I do!"

You are alive.
You see everything.

Arise, O LORD!
Punish the wicked, O God! Do not ignore the helpless!
Why do the wicked get away with despising God?
They think, "God will never call me to account."
But You see the trouble and grief they cause.
You take note of it and punish them.
The helpless put their trust in You.
You defend the orphans.

Break the arms of these wicked, evil people!
Go after them until the last one is humbled
    and brought to you.
You are King forever and ever!

The godless nations will vanish from the land.
LORD, You know the hopes of the helpless.
Surely You will hear their cries and comfort them.
You will bring justice to the orphans and the oppressed,
    so mere people can no longer terrify them.

You defend the orphans and the oppressed.
You are King forever and ever.

11

Lord, we trust You for protection.
The world says to us:

"Fly like a bird to the mountains for safety!
The wicked are stringing their bows
and fitting their arrows on the bowstrings.
They shoot from the shadows
at those whose hearts are right.
The foundations of law and order have collapsed.
What can the righteous do?"

But You, Lord, are in Your holy Temple;
You still rule from heaven.
You watch everyone closely,
examining every person on earth.
You examine both the righteous and the wicked.

You hate those who love violence.
You will rain down blazing coals and
burning sulfur on the wicked,
punishing them with scorching winds.
You are righteous, Lord, and You love justice.
The virtuous will see Your face.

You rule from heaven.
You are righteous.

12

Help, O Lord, for the godly are fast disappearing!
The faithful have vanished from the earth!

Neighbors lie to each other,
speaking with flattering lips and deceitful hearts.
Lord, cut off their flattering lips
and silence their boastful tongues.

They say, "We will lie to our hearts' content.
Our lips are our own—who can stop us?"

Lord, You reply:

"I have seen violence done to the helpless,
and I have heard the groans of the poor.
Now I will rise up to rescue them,
as they have longed for Me to do."

Lord, Your promises are pure, like silver
refined in a furnace, purified seven times over.
Therefore, Lord, we know You will protect the oppressed,
preserving them forever from this lying generation,
even though the wicked strut about,
and evil is praised throughout the land.

Your promises are pure.
You will protect the oppressed.

13

O LORD, how long will You forget us? Forever?
How long will You look the other way?
How long must we struggle with anguish in our souls,
with sorrow in our hearts every day?
How long will our enemy have the upper hand?

Turn and answer us, O LORD our God!
Restore the sparkle to our eyes, or we will die.
Don't let our enemies gloat, saying,
"We have defeated them!"
Don't let them rejoice at our downfall.

But we trust in Your unfailing love.
We will rejoice because You have rescued us.
We will sing to You because You are good to us.

You love us.
You saved us.
You are good to us.

14

The fool has said in his heart, "There is no God."
They are corrupt, they have committed abominable deeds;
There is no one who does good.

Lord, You have looked down from heaven
on the entire human race;
To see if there are any who are wise, if any seek after You.
They have all turned aside. They have all become corrupt;
There is no one who does good, not even one.

Will those who do evil ever learn?
They eat up Your people like bread
and wouldn't think of praying to You.
But terror will grip them,
for You are with those who obey You.

Evildoers frustrate the plans of the poor.
But You protect Your people.

Who will come from Mount Zion to rescue Israel?
When You restore Your people, Jacob will shout with joy,
and Israel will rejoice.

You are with us.
You are our protector.

15

Who may worship in Your sanctuary, LORD?
Who may enter Your presence on Your holy hill?

Those who lead blameless lives and do what is right,
speaking the truth from sincere hearts.

Those who refuse to gossip
or harm their neighbors
or speak evil of their friends.

Those who despise flagrant sinners,
and honor Your faithful followers,
and keep their promises even when it hurts.

Those who lend money without charging interest,
and who cannot be bribed to lie about the innocent.

Such people will stand firm forever.

You are holy.

16

Preserve us, O God, for we take refuge in You.
You are our Lord; We have no good besides You.

The godly people in the land are our true heroes.
We take pleasure in them.

Troubles multiply for those who chase after other gods.
We will not take part in their wickedness
  or even speak the names of their gods.
Nor will we take their names upon our lips.

You alone are our inheritance and our cup of blessing;
  You make our future secure.
The land You have given us is a pleasant land.
What a wonderful inheritance!
We will bless You who guides us;
  Even at night our hearts instruct us.

We constantly trust in You;
  You are at our right hand, we will not be shaken.
Therefore our hearts are glad, and our whole beings rejoice;
  Our flesh also dwells securely.

For You will not abandon our souls to Sheol;
  Nor will You allow Your Holy One to undergo decay.
You will make known to us the path of life;
  In Your presence is fullness of joy;
  In Your right hand there are pleasures forever.

You are our Lord.
You are our inheritance.
You are our ultimate joy.

17

O LORD, hear our plea for justice. Listen to our cry for help.
Pay attention to our prayer, for it comes from honest lips.
Declare us innocent, for You see those who do right.

You have tested our thoughts
and examined our hearts in the night.
You have scrutinized us and found nothing wrong.
We are determined not to sin in what we say.
We have followed Your commands,
which keep us from following cruel and evil people.
Our steps have stayed on Your path;
We have not wavered from following You.

We are praying to You
because we know You will answer, O God.
Bend down and listen as we pray.
Show us Your unfailing love in wonderful ways.
By Your mighty power You rescue those
who seek refuge from their enemies.
Keep us as the apple of Your eye.
Hide us in the shadow of Your wings.

Protect us from wicked people who attack us,
from murderous enemies who surround us.
They are without pity. Listen to their boasting!
They track us down and surround us,
watching for the chance to throw us to the ground.
They are like hungry lions,
eager to tear us apart—like young lions hiding in ambush.

You see those who do right.

Arise, O LORD!
Stand against them, and bring them to their knees!
Rescue us from the wicked with Your sword!
By the power of Your hand, O LORD,
humble those who look to this world for their reward.

But satisfy the hunger of Your treasured ones.
Make their children have plenty,
leaving an inheritance for their descendants.
Because we are righteous, we will see You.
When we awake, we will see You face to face
and be satisfied.

You are our protector.

18

We love You, Lord; You are our strength.
You are our rock, our fortress, and our savior;
You are our God, our rock, in whom we find protection.
You are our shield, the power that saves us,
and our place of safety.
We called on You, Lord. You are worthy of praise,
and You saved us from our enemies.

The ropes of death entangled us;
Floods of destruction swept over us.
The grave wrapped its ropes around us;
Death laid a trap in our path.
But in our distress, we cried out to You, Lord;
Yes, we prayed to You, our God, for help.
You heard us from Your sanctuary;
Our cry to You reached Your ears.

Then the earth quaked and trembled.
The foundations of the mountains shook;
They quaked because of Your anger.
Smoke poured from Your nostrils;
Fierce flames leaped from Your mouth.
Glowing coals blazed forth from You.
You opened the heavens and came down;
Dark storm clouds were beneath Your feet.

You are our rock.
You are our fortress.
You are our savior.
You are our shield.
You are the power that saves us.
You are our place of safety.
You are worthy of praise.

Mounted on a mighty angelic being, You flew,
soaring on the wings of the wind.
You shrouded Yourself in darkness,
veiling Your approach with dark rain clouds.
Thick clouds shielded the brightness around You
and rained down hail and burning coals.
You thundered from heaven; Your voice, Most High,
resounded amid the hail and burning coals.
You shot Your arrows and scattered Your enemies;
Great bolts of lightning flashed, and they were confused.
Then at Your command, O LORD, at the blast of Your breath,
the bottom of the sea could be seen,
and the foundations of the earth were laid bare.

You reached down from heaven and rescued us;
You drew us out of deep waters.
You rescued us from our powerful enemies,
from those who hated us and were too strong for us.
They attacked us at a moment when we were in distress,
but You, LORD, supported us.
You led us to a place of safety;
You rescued us because You delight in us.
You, LORD, rewarded us for doing right;
You restored us because of our innocence.
For we have kept Your ways, LORD;
We have not turned from You, our God, to follow evil.
We have followed all Your regulations;
We have never abandoned Your decrees.
We are blameless before You, God;
We have kept ourselves from sin.
You rewarded us for doing right.
You have seen our innocence.

You have rescued us.
You have rewarded us.

To the faithful You show Yourself faithful;
To those with integrity You show integrity.
To the pure You show Yourself pure,
but to the crooked You show Yourself shrewd.
You rescue the humble, but You humiliate the proud.
You light a lamp for us.
You light up our darkness O LORD, our God.
In Your strength we can crush an army;
With You, our God, we can scale any wall.

Your way is perfect. All Your promises prove true.
You are a shield for all who look to You for protection.
For who are You, God, except the LORD?
Who but You, our God, is a solid rock?
You arm us with strength, and You make our way perfect.

You made King David as surefooted as a deer,
enabling him to stand on mountain heights.
You trained his hands for battle and
strengthened his arm to draw a bronze bow.
You gave him Your shield of victory.
Your right hand supported him; Your help made him great.
You made a wide path for his feet to keep them from slipping.

He chased his enemies and caught them;
He did not stop until they were conquered.
He struck them down so they could not get up;
They fell beneath his feet.
You armed him with strength for the battle;
You subdued his enemies under his feet.
You placed his foot on their necks.

Your way is perfect.
Your promises prove true.

He destroyed all who hated him.
They called for help, but no one came to their rescue.
They even cried to You, but You refused to answer.
He ground them as fine as dust in the wind.
He swept them into the gutter like dirt.
You gave him victory over his accusers.
You appointed him ruler over nations;
  People he didn't even know began serving him.
As soon as they heard of him, they submitted;
  Foreign nations cringed before him.
They all lost their courage and
  came trembling from their strongholds.

You live, O LORD! Praise be to You, our Rock!
Be exalted, O God of our salvation!
You are the God who pays back those who harm us;
  You subdue the nations under us
  and rescue us from our enemies.
You hold us safe beyond the reach of our enemies;
  You save us from violent opponents.

For this, O LORD, we will praise You among the nations;
  We will sing praises to Your name.
You gave great victories to David, Your king;
  You showed unfailing love to Your anointed,
  to David and all his descendants forever.

O LORD, show Your unfailing love to us.

You live.
Your love is unfailing.

19

The heavens proclaim Your glory, God.
The skies display Your craftsmanship.
Day after day they continue to speak;
  Night after night they make You known.
They speak without a sound or word;
  Their voice is never heard.
Yet their message has gone throughout the earth,
  and their words to all the world.

You have made a home in the heavens for the sun.
It bursts forth like a radiant bridegroom after his wedding.
It rejoices like a great athlete eager to run the race.
The sun also rises at one end of the heavens
  and follows its course to the other end.
Nothing can hide from its heat.

Your law is perfect, LORD, restoring the soul;
  Your testimony is sure, making wise the simple.
Your precepts are right, rejoicing the heart;
  Your commandment is pure, enlightening the eyes.

You are the mighty Creator.
Your law is perfect.
Your testimony is sure.
Your precepts are right.
Your commandment is pure.

Reverence for You is pure, lasting forever;
    Your laws are true; Each one is fair.
They are more desirable than gold, even the finest gold;
    They are sweeter than honey,
    even honey dripping from the comb.
They are a warning to Your servant,
    a great reward for those who obey them.

How can we know all the sins lurking in our hearts?
Acquit us of these hidden faults.
Keep Your servants from deliberate sins.
Don't let them control us.
Then we will be blameless and innocent of great sin.
Let the words of our mouths
    and the meditations of our hearts
    be acceptable in Your sight,
    O Lord, our Rock and our Redeemer.

Your laws are true.
Your laws are sweeter than honey.
Your laws are a warning.
Your laws are a reward.
You are our rock.
You are our redeemer.

20

In times of trouble, LORD, answer our cry.
O God of Jacob, keep us safe from all harm.
Send us help and strengthen us.
Remember us and look favorably upon us.

Grant our hearts' desires and make all our plans succeed.
We will shout for joy when we are victorious and
raise a victory banner in Your name.
LORD, answer all our prayers.

Now we know that You rescued Your anointed king, David.
You answered him from Your holy heaven
and rescued him by Your great power.

Some boast in chariots and some in horses,
but we will boast in Your name, O LORD, our God.
Those nations will fall down and collapse,
but we will rise up and stand firm.

Give us victory, O LORD!
Answer our cry for help.

You answer our prayers.
Your name alone is powerful.

21

We rejoice in Your strength, O LORD!
We shout with joy because You give us victory
For You have given us our hearts' desire.
You have withheld nothing we requested.

You welcomed us back with success and prosperity.
You placed crowns of finest gold on our heads.
We asked You to preserve our lives,
    and You granted our request.
The days of our lives stretch on forever.
Your victory brings us great honor,
    and You have clothed us with splendor and majesty.
You have endowed us with eternal blessings
    and given us the joy of Your presence.
We trust in You, LORD.
Your unfailing love will keep us from stumbling.

You will capture all Your enemies.
Your strong right hand will seize all who hate You.
You will throw them in a flaming furnace when You appear.
You will consume them in Your anger.
Fire will devour them.
You will wipe their children from the face of the earth.
They will never have descendants.
Although they plot against You,
    their evil schemes will never succeed.
For they will turn and run
    when they see Your arrows aimed at them.

Rise up, O LORD, in all Your power.
With music and singing we celebrate Your mighty acts.

You are all powerful.

22

O God, our God, why have You abandoned us?
Why are You so far away when we groan for help?
Every day we call to You, our God, but You do not answer.
Every night we lift our voices, but we find no relief.

Yet You are holy, enthroned on the praises of Israel.
Our ancestors trusted in You, and You rescued them.
They cried out to You and were saved.
They trusted in You and were never disgraced.

But we are worms and not men and women.
We are scorned and despised by all!
Everyone who sees us mocks us.
They sneer and shake their heads, saying:

> "Are these the ones who rely on the LORD?
> Then let the LORD save them!
> If the LORD loves them so much,
> let the LORD rescue them!"

Yet You brought us safely from our mothers' wombs
and led us to trust You at our mothers' breasts.
We were thrust into Your arms at our birth.
You have been our God from the moment we were born.

Do not stay so far from us, for trouble is near,
and no one else can help us.
Your Son's enemies surrounded Him like a herd of bulls;
Fierce bulls of Bashan hemmed Him in!

You are holy.

Like lions they open their jaws against Him,
  roaring and tearing into their prey.
His life was poured out like water,
  and all His bones were out of joint.
His heart was like wax, melting within Him.
His strength dried up like sunbaked clay.
His tongue stuck to the roof of His mouth.
You laid Him in the dust and left Him for dead.
His enemies surrounded Him like a pack of dogs;
  An evil gang closed in on Him.
They pierced His hands and feet.
Though all His bones could be counted,
  His enemies stared at Him and gloated.
They divided His garments among themselves
  and threw dice for His clothing.

O Lord, do not stay far away!
You are our strength; Come quickly to our aid!
Save us from the sword;
  Spare our precious lives from these dogs.
Snatch us from the lion's jaws
  and from the horns of these wild oxen.

We will proclaim Your name to our brothers and sisters.
We will praise You among Your assembled people.
We praise You, Lord, as ones who fear You.
We honor You. We show You reverence.
For You have not ignored or belittled
  the suffering of the needy.
You have not turned Your back on them,
  but have listened to their cries for help.

You are holy.
You listen to the cries of the needy.

We will praise You in the great assembly.
We will fulfill our vows in the presence
of those who worship You.
The poor will eat and be satisfied.

All who seek You, LORD, will praise You.
Their hearts will rejoice with everlasting joy.
The whole earth will acknowledge You, LORD,
and return to You.
All the families of the nations will bow down before You.
For royal power belongs to You, LORD.
You rule all the nations.

Let the rich of the earth feast and worship.
We will bow before You, as ones who are mortal,
whose lives will end as dust.
Our children will also serve You.
Future generations will hear about Your wonders, LORD.
Your righteous acts will be told to those not yet born.
They will hear about everything You have done.

You rule all the nations.

23

You are our shepherd. We shall not want.

You make us lie down in green pastures;
You lead us beside quiet waters.

You restore our souls;
You guide us in the paths of righteousness
for Your name's sake.

Even though we walk through the valley
of the shadow of death,
We fear no evil, for You are with us;
Your rod and Your staff, they comfort us.

You prepare a table before us in the presence of our enemies;
You have anointed our heads with oil; Our cups overflow.

Surely goodness and lovingkindness
will follow us all the days of our lives,
and we will dwell in Your house forever.

You are our shepherd.
You are with us.
You are our inheritance.

24

The earth is Yours and all it contains.
The world and those who dwell in it belong to You.
For You founded it upon the seas and
established it upon the ocean currents.

Who may climb Your mountain, LORD?
And who may stand in Your holy dwelling place?
Only those whose hands and hearts are pure,
who do not worship idols and never tell lies.
They will receive Your blessing
and have a right relationship with You, LORD, our Savior.
Such people may seek You and worship in Your presence,
O God of Jacob.

LORD, let the ancient gates be opened
let the ancient doors be lifted,
that You, the King of glory, may come in!
Who is the King of glory?
You are the LORD, strong and mighty.
You are invincible in battle.

LORD, let the ancient gates be opened;
Let the ancient doors be lifted,
that You, the King of glory, may come in!
Who is this King of glory?
You are the LORD of Heaven's Armies.
You are the King of glory.

You are invincible in battle.
You are the King of Glory.

25

O Lord, we give our lives to You.
We trust in You, our God!
Do not let us be disgraced,
  or let our enemies rejoice in our defeat.
No one who trusts in You will ever be disgraced,
  but disgrace comes to those who try to deceive others.

Show us the right path, O Lord;
  Point out the road for us to follow.
Lead us by Your truth and teach us,
  for You are the God who saves us.
All day long we put our hope in You.
Remember, O Lord, Your compassion and unfailing love,
  for You have always acted in this manner.
Do not remember the rebellious sins of our youth.
Remember us in the light of Your unfailing love,
  for You are merciful, O Lord.

Lord, You are good, and You do what is right.
You teach sinners the right way to live.
You lead the humble in doing right, teaching them Your way.
You always prove faithful and reliable
  to those who follow the demands of Your covenant.
For Your name's sake, O Lord,
  pardon our iniquity, for it is great.

Who are those who fear You, Lord?
You will show us the path we should choose.
We will live in prosperity,
  and our children will inherit the land.

You are merciful.
You are good.
You do what is right.

You, LORD, are a friend to us.
You teach us Your covenant.
Our eyes are always on You, LORD,
  for You rescue us from the traps of our enemies.

Turn to us and be gracious to us,
  for we are lonely and afflicted.
Our problems go from bad to worse.
Oh, save us from them all!

Feel our pain, and see our trouble.
Forgive all our sins.
See how many enemies we have
  and how viciously they hate us!
Protect us!
Rescue our lives from them!

Do not let us be disgraced, for in You we take refuge.
May integrity and honesty protect us,
  for we put our hope in You.
O God, ransom us from all our troubles.

You are our friend.
You rescue us.
You are our hope.

26

Vindicate us, O Lord, for we have integrity,
  and we trust in You, Lord, without wavering.
Examine us, O Lord, and test us!
Evaluate our inner thoughts and motives!
For we are ever aware of Your faithfulness,
  and Your loyalty continually motivates us.

We do not associate with deceitful men
  or consort with those who are dishonest.
We hate the mob of evil men
  and do not associate with the wicked.
We maintain pure lifestyles,
  so we can appear before Your altar, O Lord,
  to give You thanks and to tell about
  all Your amazing deeds.
We love Your sanctuary, Lord,
  the place where Your glorious presence dwells.

Don't let us suffer the fate of sinners.
Don't condemn us along with murderers.
Their hands are dirty with evil schemes,
  and they constantly take bribes.

But we are not like that; We live with integrity.
Rescue us and have mercy on us!

We are safe; And we will publicly praise You, Lord.

You are faithful.

27

LORD, You are our light and our salvation,
so why should we be afraid?
You are our fortress, protecting us from danger,
so why should we tremble?
When evil men attack us,
when our enemies and foes attack us,
they stumble and fall.
Though a mighty army surrounds us,
our hearts will not be afraid.
Even if we are attacked, we will remain confident.

The one thing we ask of You, LORD—
the thing we seek most—
is to live in Your house all the days of our lives,
delighting in Your perfections
and meditating in Your temple.

For You will conceal us there when troubles come;
You will hide us in Your sanctuary.
You will place us out of reach on a high rock.
Then we will hold our heads high above our enemies
who surround us.
We will offer sacrifices in Your dwelling place
and shout for joy!
We will sing praises to You.

Hear us as we pray, O LORD. Be merciful and answer us!
Our hearts have heard You say, "Come and talk with me."
And our hearts respond, "LORD, we are coming."

You are our light.
You are our salvation.
You are our fortress.

Do not turn Your back on us.
Do not reject Your servants in anger.
You have always been our helper.
Don't leave us now;
  Don't abandon us, O God of our salvation!
Even if our fathers and mothers abandon us,
  You will hold us close.

Teach us how to live, O Lord.
Lead us along the right path,
  for our enemies are waiting for us.
Do not let us fall into their hands.
For they accuse us of things we've never done;
  With every breath, they threaten us with violence.
Yet we are confident we will see Your goodness
  while we are here in the land of the living.

We wait patiently for You, Lord.
We will be brave and courageous,
  as we wait patiently for You.

You will never abandon us.

28

We pray to You, O Lord, our Rock.
Do not turn a deaf ear to us.
For if You are silent, we might as well give up and die.
Listen to our prayer for mercy, as we cry out to You for help,
as we lift our hands toward Your holy sanctuary.
Do not drag us away with evil men,
with those who behave wickedly,
who speak friendly words to their neighbors
while planning evil in their hearts.
Give them the punishment they so richly deserve!
Measure it out in proportion to their wickedness.
Pay them back for all their evil deeds!
Give them a taste of what they have done to others.
For they do not understand Your actions or
the way You carry out justice.
You will permanently demolish them.

We praise You, Lord! For You have heard our cry for mercy.
You are our strength and shield.
We trust You with all our hearts.
You help us, and our hearts are filled with joy.
We burst out in songs of thanksgiving.
You give Your people strength.
You are a safe fortress for Your anointed king.
Save Your people!
Bless Israel, Your special possession.
Lead them like a shepherd,
and carry them in Your arms forever.

You are just.
You hear us.
You are our strength.
You help us.
You fill our hearts with joy.

29

We honor You, Lord.
We honor You for Your majesty and power.
We honor You for the glory of Your name.
We worship You, Lord, in the splendor of Your holiness.
Your shout echoes above the sea.
You, the God of glory, thunder over the mighty sea.

Your shout is powerful.
Your shout is majestic.
Your shout breaks the cedars.
You shatter the cedars of Lebanon.
You make Lebanon skip like a calf
  and Sirion like a young ox.
Your shout strikes with flaming fire.
Your shout shakes the wilderness.
You shake the wilderness of Kadesh.
Your shout bends the large trees
  and strips the leaves from the forests.

Everyone in Your temple says, "Majestic!"
You sit enthroned over the engulfing waters.
You sit enthroned as the eternal king.
You give Your people strength;
  You grant Your people security.

You are majestic.
You are the Eternal King.

30

We will praise You, LORD, for You rescued us.
You refused to let our enemies triumph over us.
O LORD our God, we cried to You for help,
  and You healed us.
You brought us up from the grave, O LORD.
You kept us from falling into the pit of death.

We will sing praise to You, LORD.
We will praise Your holy name.
For Your anger lasts only a moment,
  but Your favor lasts a lifetime!
Weeping may last through the night,
  but a shout of joy comes in the morning.
When we were prosperous, we said,
  "Nothing can stop us now!"
Your favor, O LORD, made us as secure as a mountain.
Then You turned away from us, and we were shattered.
We cried out to You, O LORD.
We begged You for mercy, saying:

  "What will You gain if we die, if we sink into the grave?
  Can the dust praise You?
  Can it tell of Your faithfulness?
  Hear us, LORD, and have mercy on us.
  Help us, O LORD."

You have turned our mourning into joyful dancing.
You have taken away our clothes of mourning
  and clothed us with joy,
  that we might sing praises to You and not be silent.
O LORD our God, we will give thanks to You forever!

You heal us.
You turn our sorrow to joy.

31

In You, LORD, we have taken refuge.
Let us never be put to shame.
Deliver us in Your righteousness.
Turn Your ear to us. Come quickly to our rescue.
Be our rock of refuge, a strong fortress to save us.
Since You are our rock and our fortress,
  for the sake of Your name, lead and guide us.
Keep us free from the trap that is set for us,
  for You are our refuge.
Into Your hands we commit our spirits.
Deliver us, LORD, our faithful God.

We hate those who cling to worthless idols;
  As for us, we trust in You, LORD.
We will be glad and rejoice in Your love,
  for You saw our affliction and
  knew the anguish of our souls.
You have not given us into the hands of the enemy
  but have set our feet in a spacious place.

Have mercy on us, LORD, for we are in distress.
Tears blur our eyes.
Our bodies and souls are withering away.
We are dying from grief; Our years are shortened by sadness.
Sin has drained our strength;
  We are wasting away from within.
We feel like David—scorned by our enemies,
  despised by our neighbors, and avoided by our friends.
We feel like when they see us on the street,
  they go the other way.
We feel ignored as if we were dead,
  as if we were broken pots.

You are our refuge.

We have heard many rumors about us,
and we are surrounded by terror.
We feel like we have enemies conspiring against us,
plotting to take our lives.
But we are trusting You, O LORD,
saying, "You are our God!"
Our future is in Your hands.
Rescue us from those who hunt us down relentlessly.
Let Your favor shine on Your servants.
In Your unfailing love, rescue us.
Don't let us be disgraced, O LORD,
for we call out to You for help.
Let the wicked be disgraced; Let them lie silent in the grave.
Silence their lying lips—those proud and arrogant lips
that accuse the godly.
How great is the goodness You have stored up
for those who fear You.
You lavish it on those who come to You for protection,
blessing them before the watching world.
You hide them in the shelter of Your presence,
safe from those who conspire against them.
You shelter them in Your presence,
far from accusing tongues.
Praise be to You, LORD, for You have
shown us the wonders of Your unfailing love.
You kept us safe when we were under attack.
In our alarm we said, "We are cut off from Your sight!"
Yet You heard our cry for mercy
when we called to You for help.
We love You, LORD, along with all Your faithful people!
You preserve those who are true to You,
but the proud You pay back in full.
We will be strong and take heart,
for our hope is in You, LORD.

You are our hope.

32

Oh, what joy for those whose disobedience is forgiven,
  whose sin is put out of sight!
Yes, what joy for those whose record You have cleared
  of guilt, whose lives are lived in complete honesty!
When we refused to confess our sin, our bodies wasted away,
  and we groaned all day long.
Day and night Your hand of discipline was heavy on us.
Our strength evaporated like water in the summer heat.

Finally, we confessed all our sins to You
  and stopped trying to hide our guilt.
We said to ourselves,
  "We will confess our rebellion to the LORD."
And You forgave us! All our guilt is gone.
Therefore, let all the godly pray to You
  while there is still time, that they may not drown
  in the floodwaters of judgment.
For You are our hiding place.
You protect us from trouble.
You surround us with songs of deliverance.

LORD, thank You for guiding us
  and teaching us in the way we should go
  and for advising us and watching over us.
We will listen to Your counsel so that we will not be
  like senseless horses or mules that have no understanding
  and need bits and bridles to keep them under control.
Many sorrows come to the wicked,
  but unfailing love surrounds those who trust You, LORD.
So we rejoice in You, LORD, and are glad, as we obey You.
We will shout for joy, for You have made our hearts pure!

You are our hiding place.
You are our guide.

33

We will sing for joy to You, LORD.
It is fitting for us to praise You.
We will praise You with music.
We will sing a new song of praise to You and sing with joy.
For Your word holds true,
  and we can trust everything You do.
You love whatever is just and good.
Your unfailing love fills the earth.

You merely spoke, and the heavens were created.
You breathed the word, and all the stars were born.
You assigned the sea its boundaries
  and locked the oceans in vast reservoirs.
Let the whole world fear You, LORD,
  and let everyone stand in awe of You.
For when You spoke, the world began!
It appeared at Your command.
You frustrate the plans of the nations
  and thwart all their schemes.
But Your plans stand firm forever.
Your intentions can never be shaken.
What joy for the nation whose God is You, LORD,
  whose people You have chosen as Your inheritance.

You watch from heaven and see the whole human race.
From Your throne You observe all who live on the earth.
You made their hearts, so You understand everything they do.
The best-equipped army cannot save a king,
  nor is great strength enough to save a warrior.
We cannot count on our greatest strengths
  or allies to give us victory.
All our skills, shrewdness, and strength cannot save us.

You are Creator of all.

But You watch over those who fear You,
those who rely on Your unfailing love.
You rescue them from death
and keep them alive in times of famine.
We put our hope in You, LORD.
You are our help and our shield.
In You our hearts rejoice, for we trust in Your holy name.
Let Your unfailing love surround us, LORD,
for our hope is in You alone.

You are our hope.
You are our help.
You are our shield.

34

We will praise You, Lord, at all times.
We will constantly speak Your praises.
We will boast only in You, Lord.
Let all who are helpless take heart.
We will tell of Your greatness
  and exalt Your name with those around us.

We pray to You, and You answer us.
You free us from all our fears.
Those who look to You for help will be radiant with joy,
  and their faces will never be ashamed.
In our desperation we prayed,
  and You listened and saved us from all our troubles.
For Your angel is a guard, who surrounds
  and defends all who fear You.

Lord, help us to taste and see that You are good.
Oh, the joys of those who take refuge in You.
Lord, teach us to fear You, for we know that all those
  who fear You will have all they need.
Even strong young lions sometimes go hungry,
  but those who trust in You will lack no good thing.
We will listen to You, Lord, teach us to fear You.
We want to live lives that are long and prosperous.
Help us keep our tongues from speaking evil
  and our lips from telling lies.
Help us turn away from evil and do good.
Give us hearts that long to search for peace
  and that work to maintain it.

You are great.
You answer us.
You free us from all our fears.

Your eyes watch over those who do right.
Your ears are open to their cries for help.
But You turn Your face against those who do evil
  and will erase their memory from the earth.
You hear Your people when they call to You for help.
You rescue them from all their troubles.
You are near to the brokenhearted
  and save those who are crushed in spirit.

The righteous person faces many troubles,
  but You come to the rescue each time.
You protect all his bones and not one of them is broken.
Calamity will surely destroy the wicked,
  and those who hate the righteous will be punished.
But You, LORD, will redeem those who serve You.
No one who takes refuge in You will be condemned.

You rescue us from all our troubles.
You are near to us when we are brokenhearted.

35

O LORD, we confess that at times we want You
to oppose those who oppose us
and fight those who fight against us,
to put on Your armor and take up Your shield,
to prepare for battle and come to our aid,
to lift up Your spear and javelin
against those who pursue us.

We confess that we want to hear You say,
"I will give You victory!"
and, at times, we want You to bring shame and disgrace
on those trying to kill us,
to turn them back and
humiliate those who want to harm us.

We confess that at times we want You
to blow them away like chaff in the wind—
a wind sent by Your angel,
to make their path dark and slippery,
with Your angel pursuing them.
We did them no wrong, but they laid a trap for us.
We did them no wrong, but they dug a pit to catch us.
This makes us want to ask You
to let sudden ruin come upon them,
to let them be caught in the trap they set for us, and
to let them be destroyed in the pit they dug for us.

But, LORD, You tell us to pray for our enemies
and that vengeance is Yours.
So, we rejoice in You, LORD.
We are glad because You rescue us.

You rescue us.

With every bone in our bodies we praise You:

"Lord, who can compare with You?
Who else rescues the helpless from the strong?
Who else protects the helpless and poor
from those who rob them?"

Malicious witnesses testify against us.
They accuse us of crimes we know nothing about.
They repay us evil for good. We are sick with despair.
Yet when they were ill, we grieved for them.
We denied ourselves by fasting for them,
but our prayers returned unanswered.
We were sad, as though they were our friends or family,
as if we were grieving for our own mothers.
But they are glad now that we are in trouble;
They gleefully join together against us.
We are attacked by people we don't even know;
They slander us constantly.
They mock us and call us names;
They snarl at us.

How long, O Lord, will You look on and do nothing?
Rescue us from their fierce attacks.
Protect our lives from these lions!
Then we will thank You in front of the great assembly.
We will praise You before all the people.
Don't let our treacherous enemies rejoice over our defeat.
Don't let those who hate us without cause
gloat over our sorrow.
They don't talk of peace;
They plot against innocent people
who mind their own business.
They shout, "Aha! Aha! With my own eyes I saw them do it!"

You vindicate us.

O LORD, You know all about this.
Do not stay silent. Do not abandon us now, O Lord.
Wake up! Rise to our defense!
Take up our case, our God and our Lord.

Declare us not guilty, O LORD our God, for You give justice.
Don't let our enemies laugh about us in our troubles.
Don't let them say:

"Look, I got what I wanted! Now I will eat them alive!"

Make those who rejoice at our troubles
be humiliated and disgraced.
Make those who triumph over us
be covered with shame and dishonor.
But give great joy to those who come to our defense.
Let them continually say:

"Great is the LORD, who delights
in blessing His servants with peace!"

Then we will proclaim Your justice,
and we will praise You all day long.

You are just.

36

Sin whispers to the wicked, deep within their hearts.
They have no fear of You at all.
In their blind conceit,
they cannot see how wicked they really are.
Everything they say is crooked and deceitful.
They refuse to act wisely or do good.
They lie awake at night, hatching sinful plots.
Their actions are never good.
They make no attempt to turn from evil.

Your unfailing love, O LORD, is as vast as the heavens.
Your faithfulness reaches beyond the clouds.
Your righteousness is like the mighty mountains.
Your justice like the ocean depths.
You care for people and animals alike, O LORD.
How precious is Your unfailing love, O God!
All humanity finds shelter in the shadow of Your wings.
You feed them from the abundance of Your own house,
letting them drink from Your river of delights.
For You are the fountain of life, the light by which we see.

Pour out Your unfailing love on those who love You;
Give justice to those with honest hearts.
Don't let the proud trample us
or the wicked push us around.
Look! Those who do evil have fallen!
They are thrown down, never to rise again.

You are the fountain of life.
Your love never fails.

37

LORD, help us to not worry about the wicked
or envy those who do wrong.
For we know that, like grass, they soon fade away,
and like spring flowers, they soon wither.
Help us to trust in You, to do good,
to dwell in the land, and to cultivate faithfulness.
Help us to delight ourselves in You. For, we know that,
when we do, You give us the desires of our hearts.
LORD, we commit our ways to You. We put our trust in You,
for we know that, when we do, You will help us.
You will make our innocence radiate like the dawn,
and the justice of our cause will shine like the noonday sun.

Teach us to rest in Your presence,
and to wait patiently for You to act.
Give us the confidence to not worry about evil people
who prosper or fret about their wicked schemes.
Please take away our anger and help us to turn from our rage.
For we know that, when we lose our tempers,
it only leads to harm.

You assure us that the wicked will be destroyed,
but those who trust in You will possess the land.
Soon the wicked will disappear.
Though we may look for them, they will be gone.
The humble will possess the land
and will live in peace and prosperity.

You give us the desires of our hearts.
You will destroy the wicked.

Though the wicked plot against the godly
  and snarl at them in defiance, You just laugh,
  for You see their day of judgment coming.

Though the wicked draw their swords and string their bows
  to kill the poor and the oppressed,
  to slaughter those who do right,
  their swords will stab their own hearts,
  and their bows will be broken.

We know that it is better to be godly and have little
  than to be evil and rich.
For the strength of the wicked will be shattered,
  but You take care of the godly.
Day by day, You take care of the innocent,
  and we will receive an inheritance that lasts forever.

We will not be disgraced in hard times;
  Even in famine we know we will have more than enough.
But the wicked will die.
LORD, Your enemies are like flowers in a field—
  they will vanish like smoke.

The wicked borrow and never repay,
  but the godly are generous givers.
Those You bless, LORD, will possess the land,
  but those You curse will surely die.

You take care of the godly.
You take care of the innocent.

You direct the steps of the godly.
You delight in every detail of our lives.
Though we stumble, we will never fall,
for You hold us by the hand.
Once we were young, and now we are old.
Yet we have never seen the godly abandoned
or our children begging for bread.
Give us the faith and courage
to give generous loans to others.
We know our children are a blessing.

Give us the wisdom and courage to turn from evil
and do good, that we may live in the land forever.
For You love justice, and You will never abandon the godly.
You will keep us safe forever,
but the children of the wicked will die.

The godly will possess the land and will live there forever.
Give us Your words that we may offer good counsel
and teach right from wrong.
Implant Your law in our hearts, LORD,
that we may never slip from our paths.
The wicked wait in ambush for the godly,
looking for an excuse to kill us.

You direct the steps of the godly.
You delight in every detail of our lives.
You hold us by the hand.
You love justice.
You will never abandon us.
You will keep us safe forever.

But You will not let the wicked succeed
   or let the godly be condemned when we are put on trial.
We put our hope in You, Lord, and strive to keep Your way.
You will honor us by giving us the land
   and allowing us to see the wicked destroyed.

We have seen wicked and ruthless people
   flourishing like a tree in its native soil.
But when we looked again, they were gone!
Though we searched for them, we could not find them!
We look at those who are honest and good.

We know that a wonderful future
   awaits those who love peace.
But the rebellious will be destroyed and have no future.
You rescue the godly,
   and You are our fortress in times of trouble.
You help us, rescuing us from the wicked.
You save us, and we find shelter in You.

You will not let the wicked succeed.
You will not let us be condemned.
You will honor us.
You will destroy the rebellious.
You will rescue us.
You are our fortress.
You help us.
You rescue us from the wicked.
You save us.
You are our shelter.

38

O Lord, don't rebuke us in Your anger
  or discipline us in Your rage!
Your arrows have struck deep,
  and Your blows are crushing us.
Because of Your anger, our whole bodies are sick;
  Our health is broken because of our sins.
Our guilt overwhelms us—it is a burden too heavy to bear.
Our wounds fester and stink because of our foolish sins.
We are bent over and racked with pain.
All day long we walk around filled with grief.
A raging fever burns within us, and our health is broken.
We are exhausted and completely crushed.
Our groans come from anguished hearts.

You know what we long for, Lord; You hear our every sigh.
Our hearts beat wildly, our strength fails,
  and we are going blind.
Our loved ones and friends stay away, fearing our disease.
Even our own families stand at a distance.
Meanwhile, our enemies lay traps to kill us.
Those who wish us harm make plans to ruin us.
All day long they plan their treachery.

But we are deaf to all their threats.
We are silent before them as ones who cannot speak.
We choose to hear nothing, and we make no reply.
For we are waiting for You, O Lord.
You must answer for us, O Lord our God.
We prayed, "Don't let our enemies gloat over us
  or rejoice at our downfall."

You hear our every sigh.

We are on the verge of collapse, facing constant pain.
But we confess our sins;
  We are deeply sorry for what we have done.
We have many aggressive enemies;
  They hate us without reason.
They repay us evil for good
  and oppose us for pursuing good.

Do not abandon us, O Lord.
Do not stand at a distance, O God.
Come quickly to help us, O Lord our savior.

You are our Savior.

39

We said to ourselves,
  "We will watch what we do and not sin in what we say.
  We will hold our tongues when the ungodly are around us."

But as we stood there in silence—not even speaking
  of good things—the turmoil within us grew worse.
The more we thought about it, the hotter we got,
  igniting a fire of words:

  "LORD, remind us how brief our time on earth will be.
  Remind us that our days are numbered—
    how fleeting our lives are.
  You have made our lives no longer
    than the width of our hands.
  Our entire lifetimes are just moments to You;
    At best, we are but breaths."

We are merely moving shadows,
  and all our busy rushing ends in nothing.
We amass riches, not knowing who will spend it.
And so, LORD, where do we put our hope?
Our only hope is in You.

You are our only hope.

Rescue us from our rebellion.
Do not let fools mock us.
We are silent before You;
  We won't say a word, for our punishment is from You.
But please stop striking us!
We are exhausted by the blows from Your hand.

When You discipline us for our sins,
  You consume like a moth what is precious to us.
We are but breaths.

Hear our prayer, O LORD!
Listen to our cries for help!
Don't ignore our tears.

For we are Your guests— travelers passing through,
  as our ancestors were before us.
Leave us alone so we can smile again
  before we are gone and exist no more.

You discipline us.

40

We waited patiently for You, Lord,
  and You turned to us and heard our cry.
You lifted us out of the pit of despair, out of the miry clay.
You set our feet upon a rock making our footsteps firm.
You have given us a new song to sing,
  a song of praise to You, our God.
Many will see and fear and will trust in You.

Oh, the joys of those who trust You, Lord,
  who have no confidence in the proud
  or in those who worship idols.
O Lord our God, You have performed many wonders for us.
Your plans for us are too numerous to list.
You have no equal.
If we tried to recite all Your wonderful deeds,
  We would never come to the end of them.

You take no delight in sacrifices or offerings.
Now that You have made us listen, we finally understand—
  You don't require burnt offerings or sin offerings.

Here we are, we have come.
We take joy in doing Your will, O God,
  for Your instructions are written on our hearts.

You turn to us.
You hear our cries.
You lift us out of despair.
You give us a new song to sing.
You have no equal.
You take no delight in sacrifices.

We have told all Your people about Your justice.
We have not been afraid to speak out,
as You, O LORD, well know.
We have not kept the good news
of Your justice hidden in our hearts;
We have talked about Your faithfulness and saving power.
We have told everyone in the great assembly
of Your unfailing love and faithfulness.
LORD, don't hold back Your tender mercies from us.
Let Your unfailing love and faithfulness always protect us.
For troubles surround us—too many to count!
Our sins pile up so high we can't see our way out.
They outnumber the hairs on our heads.
We have lost all courage.

Please, LORD, rescue us!
Come quickly, LORD, and help us.
Make those who try to destroy us
be humiliated and put to shame.
Make those who take delight in our trouble
be turned back in disgrace.
Let them be horrified by their shame, for they said,
"Aha! We've got them now!"
But may all who search for You
be filled with joy and gladness in You.
May those who love Your salvation
repeatedly shout, "The LORD is great!"
As for us, since we are poor and needy,
LORD keep us in Your thoughts.
You are our helper and our savior.
O God, do not delay.

You are faithful.
Your love is unfailing.
You are great!
You are our helper and our savior.

41

How blessed are those who treat the poor properly!
When trouble comes, LORD, You will deliver them.
Protect them and keep them alive.
Give them prosperity in the land,
  and rescue them from their enemies.
LORD, nurse them when they are sick
  and restore them to health.

O LORD, have mercy on us!
Heal us, for we have sinned against You!

We feel like David, when his enemies said nothing
  but cruel things about him,
  "When will he finally die and be forgotten?" they asked.
They came to visit and pretended to be his friends,
  but all the while they were thinking of ways to defame him,
  and when they left they would slander him.
All who hated him whispered insults
  about him to one another; and planned ways to harm him.
They said, "He has some fatal disease,
  and he will never get out of that bed."
Even his best friend, whom he trusted completely,
  one who shared meals with him, turned against him.

You care for the poor.
You are the Great Healer.

O LORD, have mercy on us and raise us up,
so we can repay our enemies with love!
We know You are pleased with us,
for our enemies do not triumph over us.
You have preserved our lives because we are innocent;
You allow us permanent access to Your presence.

We praise You, LORD, O God of Israel,
In the future and forevermore!
Amen and Amen.

You give us access to Your presence.
You are worthy of all praise.

42

As the deer pants for the water brooks,
so our souls pant for You, O God.
Our souls thirst for You—the living God;
When shall we come and appear before You, God?
Our tears have been our food day and night,
while our enemies continually taunt us,
saying, "Where is Your God?"

Our hearts are breaking as we remember how it used to be.
For we used to walk among the crowds of worshipers,
leading a great procession to the house of God,
singing for joy and giving thanks
amid the sound of a great celebration.

Why are we discouraged?
Why are our hearts so sad?
We will put our hope in You.
We will praise You again—our Savior and our God.

O God, our souls are in despair within us.
Therefore we will remember You—even from distant places.
One deep stream calls out to another
at the sound of Your waterfalls;
All Your breakers and Your waves have rolled over us.

But each day, LORD, You pour Your unfailing love upon us,
and through each night we sing Your songs,
praying to You who gives us life.

You are alive.
You are the Living Water.
You are our savior.
You are our God.
You give us life.

O God, our rock, why have You forgotten us?
Why do we wander around in grief,
  oppressed by our enemies?
Their taunts break our bones.
They scoff, "Where is Your God?"

Why are we discouraged?
Why are our hearts so sad?
We will put our hope in You.
We will praise You again—our Savior and our God.

You are our rock.
You have not forgotten us.
You are our Savior.
You are our God.

43

Declare us innocent, O God!
Defend us against these ungodly people.
Rescue us from these unjust liars.

For You are God, our only safe haven.
Why have You tossed us aside?
Why must we wander around in grief,
  oppressed by our enemies?

Send out Your light and Your truth; Let them guide us.
Let them lead us to Your holy mountain,
  to the place where You live.

There we will go to Your altar,
  to You—the source of all our joy.
We will praise You, O God, our God!

Why are we discouraged?
Why are our hearts so sad?
We will put our hope in You!
We will praise You again—our Savior and our God!

You are our only safe haven.
You are the source of all our joy.
You are our Savior.
You are our God.

44

O God, remind us what all You did in ancient times.
You drove out the pagan nations by Your power
    and gave all the land to Your people.
You crushed the people living there
    and enabled Your people to occupy it.
Your people did not conquer the land by their swords,
    and they did not prevail by their strength.
But it was Your right hand and strong arm
    and the blinding light from Your face that helped them,
    for You favored them.

You are our King and our God.
As You commanded victories for Israel,
    empowering it to push back its enemies
    and, in Your name, trample its foes,
    we will not put our trust in our abilities
    nor count on our strength to save us.
You are the one who gives us victory over our enemies;
    You disgrace those who hate us.
O God, we give glory to You all day long
    and constantly praise Your name.

But at times we feel like Your people did—

    that You had tossed them aside in dishonor;
    that You stopped leading their armies to battle;
    that You made them retreat from their enemies;
    that You allowed those who hated them
        to plunder their land;
    that You gave them up to be butchered like sheep;
    that You scattered them among the nations;

You are our King and our God.
You give us victory.

that You had sold them—Your precious people—
for a pittance, making nothing on the sale;
that You had let their neighbors mock them;
that You had allowed them to become an object of scorn
and derision to those around them;
that You had made them the butt of jokes,
with those around them shaking their heads
at them in scorn;
that they could not escape the constant humiliation,
with shame written across their faces;
that all they heard were the taunts of their mockers;
that all they saw were their vengeful enemies;
that You had crushed them and left them
in a heap of ruins overrun by wild dogs;
that You had covered them with darkness and death;
and that they were being killed every day,
being slaughtered like sheep.

Though we feel like this at times, we have not forgotten You.
We have not violated Your covenant.
Our hearts have not deserted You.
We have not strayed from Your path.
If we had forgotten Your name
or spread our hands in prayer to foreign gods,
You would surely have known it,
for You know the secrets of every heart.

Wake up, O Lord! Why do You sleep?
Get up! Do not reject us forever.
Why do You look the other way?
Why do You ignore our suffering and oppression?
We collapse in the dust, lying face down in the dirt.
Rise up! Help us!
Redeem us because of Your unfailing love.

You know the secrets of every heart.

45

Beautiful words stir our hearts.
We will recite a lovely poem about You, Jesus, the King,
for our tongues are like the pen of a skillful poet.
Jesus, You are the most handsome of all.
Gracious words stream from Your lips.
The Father Himself has blessed You forever.

Put on Your sword, O mighty warrior!
You are so glorious, so majestic!
In Your majesty, ride out to victory,
defending truth, humility, and justice.
Go forth to perform awe-inspiring deeds!
Your arrows are sharp, piercing Your enemies' hearts.
The nations fall beneath Your feet.

Your throne endures forever and ever.
You rule with a scepter of justice.
You love justice and hate evil.
Therefore the Father has anointed You, pouring out
the oil of joy on You more than on anyone else.
Myrrh, aloes, and cassia perfume Your robes.
In ivory palaces the music of strings entertains You.
You allow us to stand by Your side at Your right hand.
You will exalt us, give us honor,
and adorn us at the proper time.

Jesus:

You are the most handsome of all.
You are a mighty warrior.
You defend truth, humility, and justice.
You love justice and hate evil.
You will exalt us.

Lord, help us to listen to You
and to take to heart what You say.
Give us the courage to renounce all others
giving preference to You, over even our families.
As You delight in the beauty of our holiness,
We will honor You, for You are our Lord.
You will have others shower us with gifts,
and the wealthy will beg for our favor.

You will make us glorious in the eyes of those around us,
as You draw us to You.
What a joyful and enthusiastic procession it will be
when we enter Your palace!

We will carry on Your dynasty.
You will make us princes and princesses throughout the land.
We will bring honor to Your name in every generation.
Therefore, the nations will praise You forever and ever.

Jesus:

You are worthy of all honor and
praise forever and ever.

46

You are our refuge and strength,
always ready to help in times of trouble.
So we will not fear when earthquakes come
and the mountains crumble into the sea;
Let the oceans roar and foam.
Let the mountains tremble as the waters surge!

A river brings joy to Your city,
Your sacred home, O Most High.
You dwell in that city; It cannot be destroyed.
From the very break of day, You will protect it.
The nations are in chaos, and their kingdoms crumble!
Your voice thunders, and the earth melts!
You, the LORD of Heaven's Armies, are here with us;
You, the God of Israel, are our fortress.

Show us Your glorious works, O LORD.
Show us how You bring destruction upon the world.
You cause wars to end throughout the earth.
You break the bow and snap the spear;
You burn the shields with fire.

We will be still and know that You are God,
for You will be exalted among the nations,
and You will be exalted in the earth.
You, the LORD of Heaven's Armies, are here with us;
You, the God of Israel, are our fortress.

You are our refuge and strength.
You are here with us.
You are our fortress.
You are God.
You will be exalted among the nations.
You will be exalted in the earth.

47

We will clap our hands!
We will shout to You with joyful praise!
For You, O Lord Most High, are awesome.
You are the great King who rules the whole earth.
You subdue the nations before us,
  putting our enemies beneath our feet.
You chose our inheritance for us.

You ascended with a mighty shout.
You ascended with trumpets blaring.
We will sing praises to You, God, sing praises;
  We will sing praises to You, our King, sing praises!
For You are the King over all the earth.
We will praise You with a psalm.

You reign above the nations, sitting on Your holy throne.
The rulers of the world have gathered
  together with Your people.
For all the kings of the earth belong to You.
You are highly exalted.

You are awesome.
You rule the whole earth.

48

How great are You LORD, how deserving of praise,
in Your city, which sits on Your holy mountain!
It is high and magnificent; The whole earth rejoices to see it!
Mount Zion, the holy mountain,
is Your city—the city of the great King!
You Yourself are in Jerusalem's towers,
revealing Yourself as its defender.

The kings of the earth joined forces
and advanced against the city.
But when they saw it, they were stunned;
They were terrified and ran away.
They were gripped with terror and writhed in pain
like a woman in labor.
You destroyed them like the mighty ships of Tarshish
shattered by a powerful east wind.

We have heard of the city's glory, and long to see it ourselves—
Your city—the city of the LORD of Heaven's Armies.
It is Your city, God; You will establish her forever.

O God, we meditate on Your unfailing love
as we worship You.
As Your name deserves, O God,
You will be praised to the ends of the earth.
Your strong right hand is filled with victory.
Let the people on Mount Zion rejoice.
Let all the towns of Judah be glad because of Your justice.

You are great.
You deserve all praise.
Your love is unfailing.

Men inspected the city of Jerusalem, walked around,
    and counted the many towers.
They took note of the fortified walls
    and toured all the citadels,
    describing them for future generations.
For that is what You are like.

You are our God forever and ever,
    and You will guide us until we die.

You are our God forever and ever.
You are our guide.

49

Lord, we want to tell everyone in the world to pay attention.
The high and low, rich and poor.
We will speak wisdom and share our profound thoughts.
We listen carefully to many proverbs and
solve riddles with inspiration from music.

Why should we fear when trouble comes,
when enemies surround us?
They trust in their wealth and boast of great riches.
Yet they cannot redeem themselves from death
by paying a ransom to You.
You tell us that redemption does not come so easily,
for no one can ever pay enough
to live forever and never see the grave.
Those who are wise must finally die,
just like the foolish and senseless,
leaving all their wealth behind.

Lord, we know the grave is their eternal home,
where they will stay forever.
They may name their estates after themselves,
but their fame will not last.
You tell us they will die, just like animals.
This is the fate of fools,
though they are remembered as being wise.
Like sheep, they are led to the grave,
where death will be their shepherd.

You are our Redeemer.

You assure us that, in the morning,
  the godly will rule over them.
Their bodies will rot in the grave, far from their grand estates.
But as for us, God, You will redeem our lives.
You will snatch us from the power of the grave.

So, we will not be dismayed when the wicked grow rich
  and their homes become ever more splendid.
For when they die, they take nothing with them.
Their wealth will not follow them into the grave.
In this life, they consider themselves fortunate
  and are applauded for their success.
But they will die like all before them
  and never again see the light of day.
People who boast of their wealth don't understand;
  They will die, just like animals.
But as for us, You will redeem our lives
  and snatch us from the power of the grave.

You have power over the grave.

50

You LORD, the Mighty One, are God, and You have spoken.
You have summoned all humanity
  from where the sun rises to where it sets.
From Mount Zion, the perfection of beauty,
  You shine in glorious radiance.
You approach and are not silent.
Fire devours everything in Your way,
  and a great storm rages around You.
You call on the heavens above
  and the earth below to judge Your people.

LORD, call us to You as some of the faithful
  who made a covenant with You by sacrifice.
May the heavens proclaim Your righteousness,
  for You Yourself are judge.
We will listen as You speak.
You are God, our God!

LORD, please take pleasure in our offering—our lives.
We know You need nothing we have.
For all the animals of the forest are Yours,
  and You own the cattle on a thousand hills.
You know every bird on the mountains,
  and all the animals of the field are Yours.
If You were hungry, You would have no reason to tell us,
  for all the world is Yours and everything in it.
You don't eat the meat of bulls or drink the blood of goats.

You shine in glorious radiance.
You are not silent.
You need nothing.

Thankfulness is our sacrifice to You, O God.
Give us the strength to fulfill our vows to You—
the Most High.
We will pray to You when we are in trouble.
For we know You will rescue us and honor us.

Lord, give us hearts that long:

To recite Your decrees and obey Your covenant;
To never refuse Your discipline or
treat Your words like trash;
To never approve of thieves or
spend our time with adulterers;
To never allow our mouths to be filled with wickedness
or our tongues to be full of lies; and
To never sit around and slander our brothers—
our own mothers' sons.

Lord, if we do any of these things,
please do not remain silent.
Do not allow us to think You don't care.
Rebuke us and reveal to us our offenses against You, Lord,
so that we may confess them and repent
and so that we may not forget You and You
be inclined to tear us apart, with no one to rescue us.

Give us thankful hearts, for You say that
giving thanks is a sacrifice that truly honors You.
Please teach us to stay on Your path;
And show us Your salvation.

You will rescue us and honor us.

51

Be gracious to us, O God, according to Your lovingkindness;
According to the greatness of Your compassion,
blot out our transgressions.
Wash us thoroughly from our iniquity
and cleanse us from our sin.
For we know our transgressions, and our sin is ever before us.
Against You, You only, we have sinned
and done what is evil in Your sight,
so that You are justified when You speak
and blameless when You judge.

Behold, we were brought forth in iniquity,
and in sin our mothers conceived us.
Behold, You desire truth in the innermost being,
and in the hidden part You will make us know wisdom.
Purify us with hyssop, and we shall be clean;
Wash us, and we shall be whiter than snow.
Make us to hear joy and gladness;
Let the bones which You have broken rejoice.
Hide Your face from our sins and blot out all our iniquities.

Create in us clean hearts, O God,
and renew steadfast spirits within us.
Do not cast us away from Your presence
and do not take Your Holy Spirit from us.
Restore to us the joy of Your salvation
and sustain us with willing spirits.
Then we will teach transgressors Your ways,
and sinners will be converted to You.

You are justified when You speak.
You are blameless when You judge.
You will make us know wisdom.

Deliver us from bloodguiltiness, O God,
the God of our salvation;
Then our tongues will joyfully sing of Your righteousness.
O Lord, open our lips,
that our mouths may declare Your praise.
For You do not delight in sacrifice,
otherwise we would give it;
You are not pleased with burnt offering.
Your preferred sacrifices are broken spirits;
Broken and contrite hearts, O God, You will not despise.

By Your favor, Lord, do good to us;
Strengthen and protect our families.
Take delight in our righteous sacrifices—
our broken and contrite hearts,
our confessions, and our repentance.

You do not delight in sacrifice.
You are not pleased with burnt offering.
You delight in broken spirits and contrite hearts.

52

We will say to the wicked:

"Why do you boast about your crimes?
Don't you realize God's justice continues forever?
All day long you plot destruction.
Your tongue cuts like a sharp razor;
you're an expert at telling lies.
You love evil more than good
and lies more than truth.
You love to destroy others with your words, you liar!
But God will strike you down once and for all.
He will pull you from your home
and uproot you from the land of the living."

The righteous will see this and be amazed.
They will laugh and say:

"Look what happens to men
who do not trust in God.
They trust their wealth instead and
grow more and more bold in their wickedness."

But we are like olive trees, thriving in Your house, O God.
We will always trust in Your unfailing love.
We will praise You forever, O God, for what You have done.
We will trust in Your good name
in the presence of Your faithful people.

Your justice continues forever.
Your love is unfailing.

53

The fool has said in his heart, "There is no God."
They are corrupt, and their actions are evil;
Not one of them does good!
You look down from heaven on the entire human race
to see if anyone is truly wise, if anyone seeks You.
But no, all have turned away; All have become corrupt.

No one does good, not a single one!
Will those who do evil never learn?
They eat up Your people like bread
and wouldn't think of praying to You.
Terror will grip them,
terror like they have never known before.
You will scatter the bones of Your enemies.
You will put them to shame, for You have rejected them.

David prayed for the salvation of Israel to come out of Zion,
restoring Your people and making Israel glad.
We thank you for having done so—in Jesus.

You will scatter the bones of Your enemies.
You brought salvation out of Jerusalem.

54

Come with great power, O God, and rescue us!
Defend us with Your might.
Listen to our prayer, O God.
Pay attention to our plea.
As strangers attacked David
  and violent people tried to kill him,
  we feel like many people are against us,
  and they care nothing for You.

But You are our helper.
You keep us alive!
Make the evil plans of our enemies be turned against them.
In Your faithfulness, deliver us from them.

We will sacrifice a voluntary offering to You;
  We will praise Your name, O LORD, for it is good.
For You have rescued us from our troubles
  and helped us to triumph over our enemies.

You are our helper.
You keep us alive.
Your name is good.
You have rescued us.

55

Listen to our prayer, O God. Do not ignore our cry for help!
Please listen and answer us,
  for we are overwhelmed by our troubles.
Our enemies shout at us, making loud and wicked threats.
They bring trouble on us and angrily hunt us down.
Our hearts pound in our chests.
The terror of death assaults us.
Fear and trembling overwhelm us, and we can't stop shaking.
Oh, that we had wings like doves;
  Then we would fly away and rest!
We would fly far away to the quiet of the wilderness.
How quickly we would escape—
  far from this wild storm of hatred.

Confuse them, Lord, and frustrate their plans,
  for we see violence and conflict in the city.
Its walls are patrolled day and night against invaders,
  but the real danger is wickedness within the city.
Everything is falling apart;
  Threats and cheating are rampant in the streets.
It is not just an enemy who taunts us—
  we can bear that.
It is not just our foes who so arrogantly insult us—
  we can hide from them.
Instead, at times,
  it is our own close friends who seem to betray us.
What good fellowship we once enjoyed
  as we worshiped You together.
Also, at times, we long for death to stalk our enemies
  and for the grave to swallow them alive,
  for evil makes its home within them.
But we will call on You, God, and You will rescue us.

You will rescue us.

Morning, noon, and night we cry out in our distress,
and You hear our voices.
You ransom us and keep us safe
from the battle waged against us,
though many still oppose us.
You, God, who has ruled forever,
will hear us and humble them.
For our enemies refuse to change their ways;
They do not fear You.

We have had friends who have betrayed us
and have broken promises.
Their words were as smooth as butter,
but in their hearts was war.
Their words were as soothing as lotion,
but underneath were daggers!

We give our burdens to You, LORD,
for we know You will take care of us.
You will not permit the godly to slip and fall.
But You, O God, will send the wicked
down to the pit of destruction.
Murderers and liars will die young,
but we are trusting You to save us.

You hear our voices.
You ransom us and keep us safe.
You have ruled forever.
You will take care of us.
You will not permit the godly to slip and fall.
You will save us.

56

O God, have mercy on us, for people are hounding us.
Our enemies attack us all day long.
We are constantly hounded by those who slander us,
  and many are boldly attacking us.

But, when we are afraid, we will put our trust in You.
We praise You, God, for what You have promised.
In You, we have put our trust; We shall not be afraid.
What can mere man do to us?

They are always twisting what we say.
They spend their days plotting to harm us.
They come together to spy on us—watching our every step,
  eager to kill us.
Don't let them get away with their wickedness;
  In Your anger, O God, bring them down.

You keep track of all our sorrows.
You put our tears in Your bottle.
You have recorded each one in Your book.

Our enemies will turn back when we call to You for help.
This we know, that You are for us.
We praise You, God, for what You have promised.
Yes, LORD, we praise You for what You have promised.
In You, God, we have put our trust, we shall not be afraid.
What can man do to us?

You are for us.
You keep Your promises.

We will fulfill our vows to You, O God;
We will offer You a sacrifice of thanks.
For You have delivered our souls from death.
You have kept our feet from stumbling.
So, now, we can walk in Your presence,
O God, in Your life-giving light.

You have delivered our souls from death.
You keep our feet from stumbling.
You are worthy of all our trust.

57

Have mercy on us, O God, have mercy!
We look to You for protection.
We will hide beneath the shadow of Your wings
  until the danger passes by.
We cry out to You, O God Most High,
  to You who will fulfill Your purpose for us.
You will send help from heaven to rescue us,
  disgracing those who hound us.
You will send forth Your unfailing love and faithfulness.
We are surrounded by fierce lions
  who greedily devour human prey—
  whose teeth pierce like spears and arrows,
  and whose tongues cut like swords.
Be exalted, O God, above the highest heavens!
Make Your glory shine over all the earth.
Our enemies have set a trap for us.
We are weary from distress.
They have dug a deep pit in our path,
  but they themselves have fallen into it.
Our hearts are confident in You, O God;
  Our hearts are confident.
No wonder we can sing Your praises!
We will tell our hearts to awaken.
We will get out our instruments.
We will wake the dawn with our song.
We will thank You, Lord, among all the people.
We will sing Your praises among the nations.
For Your unfailing love is as high as the heavens.
Your faithfulness reaches to the clouds.
Be exalted, O God, above the highest heavens.
Make Your glory shine over all the earth.

You will save us from our enemies.
You are worthy of all praise.

58

LORD, the rulers of this world don't know
the meaning of the word justice.
They do not judge people fairly.
They plot injustice in their hearts
and spread violence throughout the land.
These wicked people are born sinners;
Even from birth they have lied and gone their own way.
They spit venom like deadly snakes;
They are like cobras that refuse to listen,
ignoring the tunes of the snake charmers,
no matter how skillfully they play.
Break off their fangs, O God!
Smash the jaws of these lions, O LORD!
David asked You:
to make them disappear like water into thirsty ground;
to make their weapons useless in their hands;
to make them be like snails that dissolve into slime,
like a stillborn child who will never see the sun; and
to sweep them away, both young and old,
faster than a pot heats over burning thorns.
He longed for the day when the godly
would rejoice at seeing injustice avenged
and wash their feet in the blood of the wicked.
While David asked You to exact justice on his enemies
and to destroy them, we ask that You
open the eyes of the wicked and save them.
But, like David, we all look forward to the day when, at last,
everyone will say,

"There truly is a reward for those who live for God;
Surely there is a God who judges justly here on earth."

You will judge the earth.
You will bring justice.

59

Rescue us from our enemies, O God.
Protect us from those who have come to destroy us.
Rescue us from these criminals.
Save us from these murderers.
They have set an ambush for us.
Fierce enemies are out there waiting, LORD,
 though we have not sinned or offended them.
We have done nothing wrong, yet they prepare to attack us.
Wake up! See what is happening and help us!
O LORD, God of Heaven's Armies, the God of Israel,
 wake up and punish those hostile nations.
But, though they are wicked traitors,
 please remove the veil from their eyes, O LORD.

They come out at night, snarling like vicious dogs
 as they prowl the streets.
Listen to the filth that comes from their mouths;
 Their words cut like swords.
"After all, who can hear me?" they sneer.
But LORD, You laugh at them.
You scoff at all the hostile nations.
You are our strength; We wait for You to rescue us,
 for You, O God, are our fortress.
In Your unfailing love, You will stand with us.
You will let us look down in triumph on all our enemies.

You scoff at all the hostile nations.
You are our strength, our fortress, and our refuge.
You will rescue us.
You will stand with us.

Don't kill them, for men soon forget such lessons;
    Stagger them with Your power,
    and bring them to their knees, O LORD, our shield.
Because of the sinful things they say,
    because of the evil that is on their lips,
    let them be captured by their pride,
    their curses, and their lies.

Though we may feel like asking You
    to destroy them in Your anger
    or to wipe them out completely,
    so that the whole world would know that You reign;
    Instead, God, please open their eyes to Your salvation,
    to Your Son.

Our enemies come out at night,
    snarling like vicious dogs as they prowl the streets.
They scavenge for food but go to sleep unsatisfied.

But as for us, we will sing about Your power.
Each morning we will sing with joy
    about Your unfailing love.
For You have been our refuge,
    a place of safety when we are in distress.
O our Strength, to You we sing praises,
    for You, O God, are our refuge,
    the God who shows us unfailing love.

You are our strength.
You show us unfailing love.

60

We feel like You have rejected us, O God, and broken us.
We feel like You have been angry with us.
Restore us to Your favor.
You have shaken the land and split it open.
Seal the cracks, for it trembles.
We feel like You have been very hard on us.
But You have raised a banner for those who fear You—
  a rallying point in the face of attack.
Now rescue us. Save us by Your power, and answer us.
Make promises to us, O LORD,
  like those You made to David,
  when, in Your holiness, You said:

"I WILL DIVIDE UP SHECHEM WITH JOY.
I WILL MEASURE OUT THE VALLEY OF SUCCOTH.
GILEAD IS MINE, AND MANASSEH, TOO.
EPHRAIM, MY HELMET, WILL PRODUCE MY WARRIORS,
  AND JUDAH, MY SCEPTER, WILL PRODUCE MY KINGS.
BUT MOAB, MY WASHBASIN, WILL BECOME MY SERVANT,
  AND I WILL WIPE MY FEET ON EDOM
  AND SHOUT IN TRIUMPH OVER PHILISTIA."

Who will lead us into our next battle?
Who will bring us victory over our next opponent?
Have You rejected us, O God?
Will You no longer go with us?
Oh, please help us against our enemies,
  for all human help is useless.
With Your help we will do mighty things,
  for You will trample down our adversaries.

You will lead us.
You will never reject us.
You will enable us to do mighty things.

61

O God, listen to our cry!
Hear our prayer!
From the ends of the earth, we cry to You for help
when our hearts are overwhelmed.
Lead us to the towering rock of safety,
for You are our safe refuge,
a fortress where our enemies cannot reach us.
Let us live forever in Your sanctuary,
safe beneath the shelter of Your wings!

For You have heard our vows, O God.
You have given us an inheritance
reserved for those who fear Your name.
Thank You for adding many years to the life of the King.
Thank You for making His years span the generations!
Thank You for revealing to us that He will reign forever.
Watch over Him with Your unfailing love and faithfulness.
We will sing praises to Your name forever
as we daily worship You with our lives.

You are our rock.
You are our safe refuge.
You are a fortress, protecting us from our enemies.
You have given us an inheritance of eternity with You.

62

We wait quietly before You, for our victory comes from You.
You alone are our rock and our salvation,
our fortress where we will never be shaken.
How long, O Lord, will You allow people to attack us?
To them we're just a broken-down wall or a tottering fence.
They plan to topple us from our high position.
They delight in telling lies about us.
They praise us to our faces but curse us in their hearts.
Let all that we are wait quietly before You,
for our hope is in You.
You alone are our rock and our salvation,
our fortress where we will not be shaken.
Our victory and honor come from You alone.
You are our refuge, a rock where no enemy can reach us.
We trust in You at all times.
We pour out our hearts to You, for You are our refuge.
Common people are as worthless as a puff of wind,
and the powerful are not what they appear to be.
If we weigh them on the scales,
together they are lighter than a breath of air.
We will not make our living by extortion
or put our hope in stealing.
And if our wealth increases,
we will not make it the center of our lives.
You have spoken plainly, and we have heard it many times:
Power, O God, belongs to You,
and unfailing love is Yours, O Lord.
Surely You repay all people
according to what they have done.

You alone are our rock and our salvation.
You are our fortress.
You are our refuge.
You repay all people according to what they have done.

63

O God, You are our God; We earnestly search for You.
Our souls thirst for You; Our flesh yearns for You,
in a dry and weary land where there is no water.

We have seen You in Your sanctuary
and gazed upon Your power and glory.
Your unfailing love is better than life itself;
How we praise You!
We will praise You as long as we live,
lifting up our hands to You in prayer.
You satisfy us more than the richest feast.
We will praise You with songs of joy.
We lie awake thinking of You,
meditating on You through the night.
Because You are our helper,
We sing for joy in the shadow of Your wings.
We cling to You; Your strong right hand holds us securely.

But those plotting to destroy us will come to ruin.
They will go down into the depths of the earth.
They will die by the sword and become the food of jackals.
But we will rejoice in You, God.
All who swear by You will glory in You,
while liars will be silenced.

You are our God.
Your unfailing love is better than life itself.
You hold us securely.

64

O God, listen to our complaint.
Protect our lives from our enemies' threats.
Hide us from the plots of this evil mob,
  from this gang of wrongdoers.
They sharpen their tongues like swords
  and aim their bitter words like arrows.
They shoot from ambush at the innocent,
  attacking suddenly and fearlessly.

They encourage each other to do evil
  and plan how to set their traps in secret.
"Who will ever notice?" they ask.
As they plot their crimes, they say,
  "We have devised the perfect plan!"
Yes, the human heart and mind are cunning.

But You, God, will shoot them with Your arrows,
  suddenly striking them down.
Their own tongues will ruin them,
  and all who see them will shake their heads in scorn.
Then everyone will be afraid;
  They will proclaim Your mighty acts
  and realize all the amazing things You do.

The godly will rejoice and find shelter in You, LORD.
And those who do what is right will praise You.

You hear our complaints.
You will bring justice.
You protect us.

65

What mighty praise, O God, belongs to You in Zion.
We will fulfill our vows to You, for You answer our prayers.
We must come to You.
Though we are overwhelmed by our sins,
  You forgive them all.
What joy for those You choose to bring near,
  those who live in Your holy courts.
What festivities await us inside Your holy temple.

You faithfully answer our prayers with awesome deeds,
  O God our savior.
You are the hope of everyone on earth,
  even those who sail on distant seas.
You formed the mountains by Your power
  and armed Yourself with mighty strength.
You quieted the raging oceans with their pounding waves
  and silenced the shouting of the nations.
Those who live at the ends of the earth
  stand in awe of Your wonders.
From where the sun rises to where it sets,
  You inspire shouts of joy.

You answer our prayers.
You forgive our sins.
You are our savior.
You are the hope of everyone on earth.
You formed the mountains by Your power.
You inspire shouts of joy.

You take care of the earth and water it,
  making it rich and fertile.
Your river has plenty of water;
  It provides a bountiful harvest of grain,
  for You have ordered it so.
You drench the plowed ground with rain,
  melting the clods and leveling the ridges.
You soften the earth with showers
  and bless its abundant crops.
You crown the year with a bountiful harvest;
  Even the hard pathways overflow with abundance.
The grasslands of the wilderness become a lush pasture,
  and the hillsides blossom with joy.
The meadows are clothed with flocks of sheep,
  and the valleys are carpeted with grain.
They all shout and sing for joy!

You take care of the earth.

66

We will shout joyful praises to You, O God!
We will sing about the glory of Your name!
We will tell the world how glorious You are.
How awesome are Your deeds!
Your enemies cringe before Your mighty power.
Everything on earth will worship You;
  They will sing Your praises,
  shouting Your name in glorious songs.

We will tell others to come and see what You have done,
  what awesome miracles You perform for people.
You made a dry path through the Red Sea,
  and Your people went across on foot.
We rejoice in You.
For by Your great power You rule forever.
You watch every movement of the nations;
  LORD, do not let the rebellious exalt themselves.

Let the whole world bless You, our God,
  and loudly sing Your praises.
Our lives are in Your hands,
  and You keep our feet from stumbling.
You have tested us, O God;
  You have purified us like silver.
You captured us in Your net
  and laid the burden of slavery on our backs.
Then You put a leader over us.
We went through fire and flood,
  but You brought us to a place of great abundance.

Your deeds are awesome.
You keep our feet from stumbling.
You have purified us like silver.

The psalmist promised to enter Your temple
with burnt offerings,
and to fulfill the vows he had made to You—
the sacred vows that he made when he was in deep trouble.
He promised to sacrifice burnt offerings to You—
the best of his rams as a pleasing aroma,
and a sacrifice of bulls and male goats.
With the same heart, LORD, we come before You,
with broken and contrite hearts, offering You our lives.

We will tell those who fear You to come and listen.
We will tell them what You have done for us.
For we cried out to You for help, praising You as we spoke.
If we had not confessed the sin in our hearts,
You would not have listened.
But You did listen! You paid attention to our prayers.
We praise You, God, for You did not ignore our prayers
or withdraw Your unfailing love from us.

You pay attention to our prayers.
You love us perpetually.

67

God, be merciful and bless us.
Make Your face smile with favor on us,
    that Your way may be known throughout the earth,
    Your salvation among all nations.

Let the nations praise You, O God.
Yes, let all the nations praise You.
Let the whole world sing for joy,
    because You govern the nations with justice
    and guide the people of the whole world.

Let the nations praise You, O God.
Yes, let all the nations praise You.
The earth has yielded its harvest,
    and You, God, our God, richly bless us.
Yes, You bless us,
    that people all over the world may fear You.

You govern the nations with justice.
You bless us.

68

David asked You to rise up and scatter Your enemies,
that those who hate You would run for their lives.
He asked You to blow them away like smoke,
to melt them like wax in a fire,
and to let the wicked perish in Your presence.
But we will rejoice. We will be glad in Your presence.
We will be filled with joy.
We will sing praises to You and to Your name!
We will sing loud praises to You who rides the clouds.
Your name is the Lord—We will rejoice in Your presence!

Father to the fatherless, defender of widows—
You are God, whose dwelling is holy.
You place the lonely in families;
You set the prisoners free and give them joy.
But You make the rebellious live in a sun-scorched land.

O God, when You led Your people out from Egypt,
when You marched through the dry wasteland,
the earth trembled,
and the heavens poured down rain before You,
the God of Sinai, before You, the God of Israel.
You sent abundant rain, O God, to refresh the weary land.
There Your people finally settled,
and with a bountiful harvest, O God,
You provided for Your needy people.

Your name is the Lord.
You set the prisoners free.

You give the word, and a great army brings the good news.
Enemy kings and their armies flee,
  while women divide the plunder.
Even those who lived among the sheepfolds
  found treasures—doves with wings of silver
  and feathers of gold.
You scattered the enemy kings
  like a blowing snowstorm on Mount Zalmon.

The mountains of Bashan are majestic,
  with many peaks stretching high into the sky.
And yet they look with envy at the mountain
  where You chose to live.
Surrounded by unnumbered thousands of chariots,
  You came from Mount Sinai into Your sanctuary.
When You ascended to the heights,
  You led a crowd of captives.
You received gifts from the people,
  even from those who rebelled against You.
Then You dwelt among them there.

We praise You, LORD; For You are our Savior!
For each day You carry us in Your arms.
You are a God who saves—the Sovereign LORD
  who rescues us from death.
But You will smash the heads of Your enemies,
  crushing the skulls of those who love their guilty ways.
You assured David, saying:
  "I will bring my enemies down from Bashan;
    I will bring them up from the depths of the sea.
  You, my child, will wash your feet in their blood,
    and even your dogs will get their share!"

You are our Savior.
You carry us in Your arms.
You rescue us from death.

Your procession has come into view, O God—
the procession of our God and King
as You go into the sanctuary.
Singers are in front, musicians behind;
Between them are young women playing tambourines.
We will praise You, God; For You are the source of life.
In Your procession, the little tribe of Benjamin leads the way.
Then comes a great throng of rulers from Judah
and all the rulers of Zebulun and Naphtali.

Summon Your might, O God.
Display Your power, O God, as You have in the past.
The kings of the earth are bringing tribute to You.
Rebuke these enemy nations—
these wild animals lurking in the reeds,
this herd of bulls among the weaker calves.
Make them bring bars of silver in humble tribute.
Scatter the nations that delight in war.
Let Egypt come with gifts of precious metals;
Let Ethiopia bring tribute to You.
We will sing to You, God. We will sing praises to You.
We will sing to You who rides across the ancient heavens,
Your mighty voice thundering from the sky.
We will tell everyone about Your power.
Your majesty shines down on Your people;
Your strength is mighty in the heavens.
You are awesome in Your sanctuary.
You give power and strength to Your people.

Praise be to You, O God!

You are the source of life.
You give power and strength to Your people.

69

Save us, O God, for the floodwaters are up to our necks.
Deeper and deeper we sink into the mire;
We can't find a foothold.
We are in deep water, and the floods overwhelm us.
We are exhausted from crying for help;
Our throats are parched.
Our eyes are swollen with weeping,
waiting for You, our God, to help us.
Those who hate us without cause
outnumber the hairs on our heads.
Many enemies try to destroy us with lies,
demanding that we give back what we didn't steal.

O God, You know how foolish we are;
Our sins cannot be hidden from You.
Don't let those who trust in You be ashamed because of us,
O Sovereign LORD of Heaven's Armies.
Don't let us cause them to be humiliated, O God of Israel.
For we endure insults for Your sake;
Humiliation is written all over our faces.
Even our own brothers pretend they don't know us;
They treat us like strangers.

LORD, give us a passion for Your house that consumes us,
And, should the insults of those who insult You fall on us,
LORD, give us the faith we need to endure.
When we weep and fast and feel like those around us
are scoffing at us, or when we appropriately show sorrow
and feel like those around us are making fun of us
or gossiping about us,
LORD, give us wisdom to trust in You more.

You know us.
You give us faith.

We will keep praying to You, Lord,
  hoping You will show us favor.
In Your unfailing love, O God,
  answer our prayers with Your sure salvation.
Rescue us from the mud; Don't let us sink any deeper!
Save us from those who hate us,
  and pull us from these deep waters.
Don't let the floods overwhelm us,
  or the deep waters swallow us,
  or the pit of death devour us.

Answer our prayers, O Lord,
  for Your unfailing love is wonderful.
Take care of us, for Your mercy is so plentiful.
Don't hide from Your servants;
  Answer us quickly, for we are in deep trouble!
Come and redeem us; Free us from our enemies.

You know of our shame, scorn, and disgrace.
You see all that our enemies are doing.
Their insults have broken our hearts, and we are in despair.
If only one person would show some pity;
  If only one would turn and comfort us.
But instead, like David, we feel like they are out to get us.

Your love is unfailing.
Your salvation is sure.
Your unfailing love is wonderful.
Your mercy is plentiful.

At times, we confess, we are inclined to pray, as David did:

"Let the bountiful table set before them
    become a snare and their prosperity become a trap.
Let their eyes go blind so they cannot see,
    and make their bodies shake continually.
Pour out Your fury on them;
    Consume them with Your burning anger.
Let their homes become desolate
    and their tents be deserted.
To the one You have punished,
    they add insult to injury;
    They add to the pain of those You have hurt.
Pile their sins up high, and don't let them go free.
Erase their names from the Book of Life;
    Don't let them be counted among the righteous."

We are suffering and in pain.
Rescue us, O God, by Your saving power.
We will praise Your name with singing,
    and we will honor You with thanksgiving.
For this will please You more than sacrificing cattle,
    more than presenting a bull with its horns and hooves.
The humble will see You at work and be glad.
Let all who seek Your help be encouraged.
For You hear the cries of the needy;
    You do not despise Your imprisoned people.
We will praise You, as will all heaven and earth,
    and the seas and all that move in them.
For You will save Jerusalem and rebuild the towns of Judah.
Your people will live there and settle in their own land.
The descendants of those who obey You will inherit the land,
    and those who love You will live there in safety.

You are our rescuer.
You hear the cries of the needy.

70

Please, God, rescue us! Come quickly, LORD, and help us.
Make those who try to kill us be humiliated
and put to shame.
Make those who take delight in our trouble
be turned back in disgrace.
Let them be horrified by their shame,
for they said, "Aha! We've got them now!"

But make all who search for You
be filled with joy and gladness in You.
Make those who love Your salvation
repeatedly shout, "God is great!"
But as for us, we are poor and needy;
Please hurry to our aid, O God.

You are our helper and our savior; O LORD, do not delay.

You are our helper.
You are our savior.

71

O LORD, we have come to You for protection;
Don't let us be disgraced.
Save us and rescue us, for You do what is right.
Turn Your ear to listen to us and set us free.
Be our rock of safety where we can always hide.
Give the order to save us,
for You are our rock and our fortress.
God, rescue us from the power of the wicked,
from the clutches of cruel oppressors.
O LORD, You alone are our hope.
We've trusted You, O LORD, from childhood.
Yes, You have been with us from birth;
From our mothers' wombs You have cared for us.
No wonder we are always praising You!

Our lives are an example to many,
because You have been our strength and protection.
That is why we can never stop praising You;
We declare Your glory all day long.
Don't set us aside when we get old.
Don't abandon us when our strength is failing.
We feel like our enemies are whispering against us,
like they are plotting together to kill us,
saying, "God has abandoned them. Let's go and get them,
for no one will help them now."

You do what is right.
You are our rock and our fortress.
You alone are our hope.
You have cared for us from birth.

O God, don't stay away. God, please hurry to help us.
Bring disgrace on our accusers and destruction to their plans.
Humiliate and shame those who want to harm us.
But we will keep on hoping for Your help;
  We will praise You more and more.
We will tell everyone about Your righteousness.
All day long we will proclaim Your saving power,
  though we are not skilled with words.
We will praise Your mighty deeds, O Sovereign LORD.
We will tell everyone that You alone are just.

O God, You have taught us from earliest childhood,
  and we constantly tell others
  about the wonderful things You do.
As we get old and gray, do not abandon us, O God.
Let us proclaim Your power to this new generation,
  Your mighty miracles to all who come after us.

Your righteousness, O God, reaches to the highest heavens.
You have done such wonderful things.
Who can compare with You, O God?
You have allowed us to suffer much hardship,
  but You will restore us to life again
  and lift us up from the depths of the earth.
You will restore us to even greater honor
  and comfort us once again.

You alone are just.
You will restore us.

Then we will praise You with music,
because You are faithful to Your promises, O God.
We will sing praises to You, O Holy One of Israel.
We will shout for joy and sing Your praises,
for You have ransomed us.
We will tell about Your righteous deeds all day long,
for everyone who tried to hurt us
has been shamed and humiliated.

You are faithful to Your promises.
You have ransomed us.

72

Give Your love of justice and righteousness
 to Your Son, O God.
Help Him judge Your people in the right way,
 with the poor always being treated with justice.
May the mountains yield prosperity for all,
 and may the hills be fruitful.
Help Him to defend the poor,
 rescue the children of the needy,
 and crush their oppressors.
May they fear You as long as the sun shines,
 as long as the moon remains in the sky.
Yes, forever!

When He comes down like spring rain
 on freshly cut grass,
 like the showers that water the earth,
 may all the godly flourish during His reign.

Make there be abundant prosperity until the moon is no more.
He will reign from sea to sea,
 and from the Euphrates River to the ends of the earth.
Desert nomads will bow before Him;
 His enemies will fall before Him in the dust.
The western kings of Tarshish
 and other distant lands will bring Him tribute.
The eastern kings of Sheba and Seba will bring Him gifts.
All kings will bow before Him,
 and all nations will serve Him.

Your Son will rule all.

He will rescue the poor when they cry to Him;
He will help the oppressed,
who have no one to defend them.
He feels pity for the weak and the needy,
and He will rescue them.
He will redeem them from oppression and violence,
for their lives are precious to Him.

Long live the King! May the gold of Sheba be given to Him.
May the people always pray for Him
and bless Him all day long.
May there be abundant grain throughout the land,
flourishing even on the hilltops.
May the fruit trees flourish like the cedars of Lebanon,
and may the people thrive like grass in a field.
The King's name will endure forever;
It will continue as long as the sun shines.
All nations will be blessed through Him
and will bring Him praise.

We praise You, LORD God, the God of Israel,
who alone does such wonderful things.
We praise Your glorious name forever!
May the whole earth be filled with Your glory.
Amen and amen!

You defend the poor.
You rescue the children of the needy.
You crush the oppressor.
Your name will endure forever.

73

Truly You are good to Your people,
   to those whose hearts are pure.
But as for us, we almost lost our footing.
Our feet almost slipped out from under us.
For we envied the proud
   when we saw them prosper despite their wickedness.
They seem to live such painless lives;
   Their bodies are so healthy and strong.
They don't have troubles like other people;
   They're not plagued with problems like everyone else.
Arrogance is their necklace and violence their clothing.
Their eyes bulge with abundance;
   They have everything their hearts could ever wish for!
They scoff and speak only evil;
   In their pride they seek to crush others.
They boast against the very heavens,
   and their words strut throughout the earth.
And so the people are dismayed and confused,
   drinking in all their words.
"What does God know?" they ask.
"Does the Most High even know what's happening?"
Look at these wicked people—
   enjoying a life of ease while their riches multiply.

Did we keep our hearts pure for nothing?
Did we keep ourselves innocent for no reason?
We get nothing but trouble all day long;
   Every morning brings us pain.
If we had really spoken this way to others,
   We would have been traitors to Your people.
So we tried to understand why the wicked prosper.
But what a difficult task it is!

You will judge the wicked.

Then we went into Your sanctuary, O God,
  and we finally understood the destiny of the wicked.
Truly, You put them on a slippery path
  and send them sliding over the cliff to destruction.
In an instant they are destroyed,
  completely swept away by terrors.
When You arise, O Lord,
  You will laugh at their silly ideas
  as a person laughs at dreams in the morning.

Then we realized that our hearts were bitter,
  and we were all torn up inside.
We were so foolish and ignorant—
  We must have seemed like senseless animals to You.
Yet we still belong to You; You hold our right hands.
You guide us with Your counsel,
  leading us to a glorious destiny.
Whom have we in heaven but You?
And besides You, we desire nothing on earth.
Our flesh and our hearts may fail,
  but You are the strength of our hearts
  and our portion forever.

Those who desert You will perish,
  for You destroy those who abandon You.
But as for us, how good it is to be near You!
We have made You our refuge,
  and we will tell everyone
  about the wonderful things You do.

You are our guide.
You are our hearts' desire.
You are our refuge.

74

O God, why does it feel like
You have rejected us for so long?
Why does Your anger seem so intense against us?
Remember that we are Yours and that You chose us long ago,
redeemed as Your own special possessions!

Remember us like You remembered Jerusalem,
Your home here on earth,
when it was laid to ruins
after the enemy destroyed Your sanctuary.
There Your enemies shouted their victorious battle cries;
There they set up their battle standards.
They swung their axes like woodcutters in a forest.
With axes and picks, they smashed the carved paneling.
They burned Your sanctuary to the ground.
They defiled the place that bears Your name.
Then they thought, "Let's destroy everything!"
So they burned down all the places
where You were worshiped.

At times we feel as though
we no longer see Your miraculous signs.
All the prophets are gone,
and no one can tell us when it will end.
How long, O God, will You allow our enemies to insult You?
Will You let them dishonor Your name forever?
Why do You hold back Your strong right hand?
At times we long for You to unleash Your powerful fist
and destroy them;
But we know that You call us to love them
and pray for them.

You chose us long ago.

You, O God, are our king from ages past,
  bringing salvation to the earth.
You split the sea by Your strength
  and smashed the heads of the sea monsters.
You crushed the heads of Leviathan
  and let the desert animals eat him.
You caused the springs and streams to gush forth,
  and You dried up rivers that never run dry.
Both day and night belong to You;
  You made the starlight and the sun.
You set the boundaries of the earth,
  and You made both summer and winter.
See how these enemies insult You, Lord.
A foolish nation has dishonored Your name.
Don't let these wild beasts destroy Your turtledoves.
Don't forget Your suffering people forever.

Remember Your covenant promises,
  for the land is full of darkness and violence!
Don't let the downtrodden be humiliated again.
Instead, let the poor and needy praise Your name.

Arise, O God, and defend Your cause.
Remember how these fools insult You all day long.
Don't overlook what Your enemies have said
  or their growing uproar.

You are our king.
You bring salvation to the earth.
You rule over all nature.
You created everything.

75

We give thanks to You, O God!
We give thanks because You are near.
Men declare Your wondrous works.

You have said:

"At the time I have planned,
I will bring justice against the wicked.
When the earth quakes and its people live in turmoil,
I am the one who keeps its foundations firm.
I warned the proud, 'Stop your boasting!'
I told the wicked, 'Don't raise your fists!
Don't raise your fists in defiance at the heavens
or speak with such arrogance.'"

For no one on earth—from east or west,
or even from the wilderness—should raise a defiant fist.
But You alone are the judge;
You put down one and exalt another.
For You, LORD, hold a cup in Your hand
that is full of foaming wine mixed with spices.
You pour out the wine in judgment,
and all the wicked must drink it, draining it to the dregs.

But as for us, we will always proclaim what You have done;
We will sing praises to You, the God of Jacob.
For You say, "I will break the strength of the wicked,
but I will increase the power of the godly."

You are near.
You will bring justice to the wicked.
You alone are judge.

76

You were honored in Judah; Your name was great in Israel.
Jerusalem is where You chose to live;
  Mount Zion is what You called Your home.
There You broke fiery arrows of the enemy
  and the shields and swords and weapons of war.

You are resplendent,
  more majestic than the mountains of prey.
Israel's boldest enemies were plundered.
They slept their last sleep.
No warrior could lift a hand against Your people.
At Your rebuke, O God of Jacob,
  their horses and chariots lay still.

No wonder You are greatly feared!
Who can stand before You when Your anger explodes?
From heaven You sentenced Your enemies;
  The earth trembled and stood silent before You.
You stand up to judge those who do evil, O God,
  and to rescue the oppressed of the earth.
Human defiance only enhances Your glory,
  for You use it as a weapon.

We will make vows to You, O LORD, our God,
  and we will keep them.
Let everyone bring tribute to You, the One to be feared.
For You break the spirit of rulers,
  and the kings of the earth fear You.

Your name is great.
You are resplendent.
You judge those who do evil.
You are to be feared.
You break the spirit of rulers.

77

We cry out to You; Yes, we shout.
Oh, that You would listen to us!
When we were in deep trouble, we searched for You, LORD.
All night long we prayed, with hands lifted toward heaven,
  but our souls were not comforted.
We think of You, God, and we moan,
  overwhelmed with longing for Your help.

You don't let us sleep. We are too distressed even to pray!
We think of the good old days, long since ended,
  when our nights were filled with joyful songs.
We search our souls and ponder the difference now.
Have You rejected us forever?
Will You never again be kind to us?
Is Your unfailing love gone forever?
Have Your promises permanently failed?
Have You forgotten to be gracious?
Have You slammed the door on Your compassion?
And we said, "This is our fate;
  The Most High has turned His hand against us."
But then we recall all You have done, O LORD;
  We remember Your wonderful deeds of long ago.
They are constantly in our thoughts.
We cannot stop thinking about Your mighty works.

O God, Your ways are holy.
Is there any god as mighty as You?
You are the God of great wonders!
You demonstrate Your awesome power among the nations.

Your ways are holy.
You are the God of great wonders.

By Your strong arm, You redeemed Your people,
the descendants of Jacob and Joseph.
When the Red Sea saw You, O God,
its waters looked and trembled!
The sea quaked to its very depths.
The clouds poured down rain;
The thunder rumbled in the sky.

Your arrows of lightning flashed.
Your thunder roared from the whirlwind;
The lightning lit up the world!
The earth trembled and shook.
Your road led through the sea,
Your pathway through the mighty waters—
a pathway no one knew was there!
You led Your people along that road like a flock of sheep,
with Moses and Aaron as their shepherds.

You redeem Your people.

78

We will listen to Your truth,
Your words, Your sayings of old,
which have been passed down for generations.
We will teach others hidden lessons from the past—
We will not hide these truths from our children
but will tell the next generation
about Your glorious deeds,
about Your power and Your mighty wonders.
For You issued Your laws to Jacob;
You gave Your instructions to Israel.

You commanded our ancestors
to teach them to their children,
so the next generation might know them—
even the children not yet born—
and they in turn will teach their own children.
So each generation should put its confidence in You
and not forget Your glorious miracles
but obey Your commands.
Then they will not be like their ancestors—
stubborn, rebellious, and unfaithful,
refusing to give their hearts to You.

The warriors of Ephraim, though armed with bows,
turned their backs and fled on the day of battle.
They did not keep Your covenant
and refused to live by Your instructions.
They forgot what You had done—
the great wonders You had shown them,
the miracles You did for their ancestors
on the plain of Zoan in the land of Egypt.

You've done great and miraculous things throughout history.

For You divided the sea and led them through,
making the water stand up like walls!
In the daytime, You led them by a cloud,
and all night by a pillar of fire.
You split open the rocks in the wilderness
to give them water, as from a gushing spring.
You made streams pour from the rock,
making the waters flow down like a river!

Yet they kept on sinning against You,
rebelling against You, the Most High in the desert.
They stubbornly tested You in their hearts,
demanding the foods they craved.
They even spoke against You, saying:
"God can't give me food in the wilderness.
Yes, He can strike a rock so water gushes out,
but He can't give His people bread and meat."

When You heard them, You were furious.
The fire of Your wrath burned against Jacob.
Yes, Your anger rose against Israel,
for they did not believe You or trust You to care for them.
But You commanded the skies to open;
You opened the doors of heaven.
You rained down manna for them to eat;
You gave them bread from heaven.
They ate the food of angels!
You gave them all they could hold.
You released the east wind in the heavens
and guided the south wind by Your mighty power.

You've done great and miraculous things throughout history.

You rained down meat as thick as dust—
birds as plentiful as the sand on the seashore!
You caused the birds to fall within their camp
and all around their tents.
The people ate their fill. You gave them what they craved.
But before they satisfied their craving,
while the meat was yet in their mouths,
Your anger rose against them,
and You killed their strongest men.
You struck down the finest of Israel's young men.

But in spite of this, the people kept sinning.
Despite Your wonders, they refused to trust You.
So You ended their lives in failure, their years in terror.
When You began killing them, they finally sought You.
They repented and took You seriously.
Then they remembered that You were their rock,
that You were their redeemer.
But all they gave You was lip service;
They lied to You with their tongues.

Their hearts were not loyal to You.
They did not keep Your covenant.
Yet You were merciful and forgave their sins
and did not destroy them all.
Many times You held back Your anger
and did not unleash Your fury!
For You remembered that they were merely mortal,
gone like a breath of wind that never returns.

You've done great and miraculous things throughout history.

How often they rebelled against You in the wilderness
  and grieved Your heart in that dry wasteland.
Again and again they tested Your patience
  and provoked You, the Holy One of Israel.
They did not remember Your power
  and how You rescued them from their enemies.

They did not remember Your miraculous signs in Egypt,
  Your wonders on the plain of Zoan.
For You turned their rivers into blood,
  so no one could drink from the streams.
You sent vast swarms of flies to consume them
  and hordes of frogs to ruin them.
You gave their crops to caterpillars;
  Their harvest was consumed by locusts.
You destroyed their grapevines with hail
  and shattered their sycamore-figs with sleet.
You abandoned their cattle to the hail,
  their livestock to bolts of lightning.
You loosed on them Your fierce anger—
  all Your fury, rage, and hostility.
You dispatched against them a band of destroying angels.
You turned Your anger against them;
  You did not spare the Egyptians' lives
  but ravaged them with the plague.
You killed the oldest son in each Egyptian family,
  the flower of youth throughout the land of Egypt.

You've done great and miraculous things throughout history.

But You led Your own people like a flock of sheep,
guiding them safely through the wilderness.
You kept them safe so they were not afraid;
But the sea covered their enemies.
You brought them to the border of Your holy land,
to this land of hills You had won for them.
You drove out the nations before them;
You gave them their inheritance by lot.
You settled the tribes of Israel into their homes.

But they kept testing and rebelling against You,
the Most High God. They did not obey Your laws.
They turned back and were as faithless as their parents.
They were as undependable as a crooked bow.
They angered You by building shrines to other gods;
They made You jealous with their idols.
When You heard them, You were very angry,
and You completely rejected Israel.
Then You abandoned Your dwelling at Shiloh,
the Tabernacle where You had lived among the people.

You allowed the Ark of Your might to be captured;
You surrendered Your glory into enemy hands.
You gave Your people over to be butchered by the sword,
because You were so angry with Your own people—
Your special possession.
Their young men were killed by fire;
Their young women died
before singing their wedding songs.
Their priests were slaughtered,
and their widows could not mourn their deaths.

You've done great and miraculous things throughout history.

Then You rose up as though waking from sleep,
like a warrior aroused from a drunken stupor.
You routed Your enemies and sent them to eternal shame.
But You rejected Joseph's descendants;
You did not choose the tribe of Ephraim.
You chose instead the tribe of Judah,
and Mount Zion, which You loved.

There You built Your sanctuary as high as the heavens,
as solid and enduring as the earth.
You chose Your servant David,
calling him from the sheep pens.
You took David from tending the ewes and lambs
and made him the shepherd of Jacob's descendants—
Your own people, Israel.
You cared for them with a true heart
and led them with skillful hands.

You've done great and miraculous things throughout history.

79

O God, pagan nations conquered Your land,
Your special possession.
They defiled Your holy temple
and made Jerusalem a heap of ruins.
They left the bodies of Your servants
as food for the birds of heaven.
The flesh of Your godly ones
became food for the wild animals.
Blood flowed like water all around Jerusalem;
No one was left to bury the dead.
Your people were mocked by their neighbors,
making them feel like objects of scorn and derision
to those around them.

O Lord, at times we feel the same way and want to ask:

"How long will You be angry with us? Forever?
How long will Your jealousy burn like fire?"

At times, we wish You would pour out Your wrath
on nations that refuse to acknowledge You—
on kingdoms that do not call upon Your name.
For they devoured Your people Israel,
making the land a desolate wilderness.

Do not hold us guilty for the sins of our ancestors!
Let Your compassion quickly meet our needs,
for we are on the brink of despair.
Help us, O God of our salvation!
Help us for the glory of Your name.
Save us and forgive our sins for the honor of Your name.

You are patient, not wanting any to perish
but for all to come to repentance.

Why should pagan nations be allowed to scoff,
  asking, "Where is their God?"
We confess, at times we want to see Your vengeance
  against the nations,
  for they have spilled the blood of Your servants.
Listen to the moaning of the prisoners.
Demonstrate Your great power
  by saving those condemned to die.

O Lord, we long to see Your justice,
  for you to pay back such nations seven times
  for the scorn they have hurled at You.
But we know, LORD, that this will occur in Your time.
Then we, Your children, the sheep of Your pasture,
  will thank You forever and ever,
  praising Your greatness from generation to generation.

You are patient, not wanting any to perish
but for all to come to repentance.

80

Please listen, O Shepherd of Israel,
You who lead Your people like a flock.
O God, enthroned above the cherubim,
display Your radiant glory
to Ephraim, Benjamin, and Manasseh.
Show us Your mighty power.
Come to rescue us!

Turn us again to You, O God.
Make Your face shine down upon us.
Only then will we be saved.
O Lord God of Heaven's Armies,
at times we feel like You are angry with our prayers.
We feel like You have fed us with sorrow
and made us drink tears by the bucketful.
We feel like You have made us the scorn of neighbors
and like our enemies treat us as jokes.

Turn us again to You, O God of Heaven's Armies.
Make Your face shine down upon us.
Only then will we be saved.
You brought Your people from Egypt like a grapevine;
You drove away the pagan nations and planted it.
You cleared the ground before it,
and it took root and filled the land.
The mountains were covered with its shadow,
and its branches covered the mighty cedars.
It spread its branches west to the Mediterranean Sea
and its shoots east to the Euphrates River.

You lead Your people.
You are enthroned above the cherubim.

But then, You broke down its walls
so that all who passed by could steal its fruit. Why?
The wild boar from the forest could devour it,
and the wild animals could feed on it.
At times, we feel just like this—
like You prepared a wonderful place for us,
set us up for success, then pulled back,
leaving us exposed.

Come back, we beg You, O God of Heaven's Armies.
Look down from heaven and see our plight.
Care for this grapevine that You Yourself have planted,
and for the children You have strengthened for Yourself.
For we feel chopped up and burned by our enemies.
We confess that, at times, we wish they would perish
at the sight of Your frown.
Strengthen the people of Your right hand,
the sons of man whom You made strong for Yourself.
Then we will never abandon You again.
Revive us so we can call on Your name once more.

Turn us again to You, O Lord God of Heaven's Armies.
Make Your face shine down upon us.
Only then will we be saved.

You are the God of heaven's armies.
You are our only means of salvation.

81

We will sing praises to You, O God, our strength.
We will sing to You, the God of Jacob.
You commanded Your people:
to sing and play the tambourine,
to play the sweet lyre and the harp,
to blow the ram's horn at new moon,
and again at full moon to call a festival!

For this was required by the decrees of Israel;
It was a regulation of Yours, O God of Jacob.
You made it a law for Israel
when You attacked Egypt to set them free.

You told Your people, in an unknown voice:

"Now I will take the load from your shoulders;
I will free your hands from their heavy tasks.
You cried to Me in trouble, and I saved you;
I answered out of the thundercloud
and tested your faith
when there was no water at Meribah.

Listen to Me, O My people,
while I give you stern warnings.
O Israel, if you would only listen to Me!
You must never have a foreign god;
You must not bow down before a false god.
For it was I, the Lord your God,
who rescued you from the land of Egypt.
Open your mouth wide,
and I will fill it with good things.

You are our strength.

But no, My people wouldn't listen.
Israel did not want Me around.
So I let them follow their own stubborn desires,
    living according to their own ideas.
Oh, that My people would listen to Me.
Oh, that Israel would follow Me and walk in My paths.
How quickly I would then subdue their enemies.
How soon My hands would be upon their foes.
Those who hate Me would cringe before Me;
    They would be doomed forever.
But I would feed you with the finest wheat.
I would satisfy you with wild honey from the rock."

Speak to us, Lord; For we long to listen to You.

You are the giver of good things.

82

You preside over heaven's court.
You pronounce judgment on the heavenly beings.
How long will You hand down seemingly unjust decisions
  by favoring the wicked?

Give justice to the poor and the orphan;
  Uphold the rights of the oppressed and the destitute.
Rescue the poor and helpless;
  Deliver them from the grasp of evil people.

But these oppressors know nothing; They are so ignorant!
They wander about in darkness,
  while the whole world is shaken to the core.
You called Your people gods,
  as they were children of the Most High.
But You reminded them that they would die
  like all other mere mortals.

Rise up, O God, and judge the earth,
  for all the nations belong to You.

You rule over everything.
You care for the poor and the orphan.

83

O God, do not be silent!
Do not be deaf.
Do not be quiet, O God.
Don't You hear the uproar of Your enemies?
Don't You see that Your arrogant enemies are rising up?
They devise crafty schemes against Your people;
  They conspire against Your precious ones.

"Come," they say, "let me wipe out Israel as a nation.
  We will destroy the very memory of its existence."
Yes, this was their unanimous decision.
They signed a treaty as allies against You—
  the Edomites and Ishmaelites; Moabites and Hagrites;
  Gebalites, Ammonites, and Amalekites;
  and people from Philistia and Tyre.
Assyria joined them, too,
  and allied with the descendants of Lot.

At times we want You to do to those
  who terrorize Your people as You did to the Midianites
  and as You did to Sisera and Jabin at the Kishon River.
They were destroyed at Endor,
  and their decaying corpses fertilized the soil.
At times we want their mighty nobles to die
  as Oreb and Zeeb did;
  And for all their princes to die like Zebah and Zalmunna.
For they said, "Let me seize for my own use
  these pasturelands of God!"

You avenge Your people.

O God, scatter them like tumbleweed,
like chaff before the wind!
As a fire burns a forest and as a flame sets mountains ablaze,
chase them with Your fierce storm;
Terrify them with Your tempest.
Utterly disgrace them
until they submit to Your name, O LORD.
Though we want them to be ashamed and terrified forever
and to die in disgrace, save them LORD.
Then the world will learn that You alone are called the LORD,
that You alone are the Most High,
supreme over all the earth.

You alone are the LORD Most High.

84

How lovely is Your dwelling place,
O LORD of Heaven's Armies.
Our souls longed and even yearned for Your courts.
With our whole being, body and soul,
We will shout joyfully to You, the living God.
Even the sparrow finds a home,
and the swallow builds her nest
and raises her young at a place near Your altar,
O LORD of Heaven's Armies, our King and our God!

What joy for those who can live in Your house,
always singing Your praises.
What joy for those whose strength comes from You, O LORD,
who have set their minds on their journey with You.
When they walk through the Valley of Weeping,
it will become a place of refreshing springs.
The autumn rains will clothe it with blessings.
They will continue to grow stronger,
and each of them will appear before You.

O LORD God of Heaven's Armies, hear our prayer.
Listen, O God of Jacob.
O God, look with favor upon our leaders.
Show favor to those You have established.

You are the living God.
You are our King and our God.

A day in Your courts is better than a thousand elsewhere!
We would rather stand at the threshold
    of the house of our God
    than dwell in the homes of the wicked.
For You are our sun and shield.
You give us grace and glory.
No good thing do You withhold
    from those who do what is right.
O LORD of Heaven's Armies,
    what joy for those who trust in You.

You are our sun and shield.
You give us grace and glory.
You give us good things.

85

Lord, You poured out blessings on us!
You restored our fortunes.
You forgave our guilt—yes, You covered all our sins.
You held back Your fury.
You kept back Your blazing anger.

Now restore us again, O God of our salvation.
Put aside Your anger against us once more.
Will You be angry with us always?
Will You prolong Your wrath to all generations?
Won't You revive us again, so we can rejoice in You?
Show us Your unfailing love, O Lord,
and grant us Your salvation.

We listen carefully to what You are saying,
for You speak peace to us.
But let us not return to our foolish ways.
Surely Your salvation is near to those who fear You,
so our world will be filled with Your glory.

Unfailing love and truth have met together.
Righteousness and peace have kissed!
Truth springs up from the earth,
and righteousness smiles down from heaven.
Yes, You pour down Your blessings.
Our work will be productive.
Righteousness goes as a herald before You,
preparing the way for Your steps.

You speak peace to us.
You pour down Your blessings on us.

86

Bend down, O LORD, and hear our prayer;
  Answer us, for we need Your help.
Protect us, for we are devoted to You.
Save us, for we serve You and trust You. You are our God.
Be merciful to us, O LORD,
  for we are calling on You constantly.
Give us happiness, O LORD, for we give ourselves to You.
O LORD, You are so good, so ready to forgive,
  so full of unfailing love for all who ask for Your help.
Listen closely to our prayer, O LORD; Hear our urgent cry.
We will call to You whenever we are in trouble,
  and You will answer us.

No pagan god is like You, O LORD.
None can do what You do!
All the nations You made will come
  and bow before You, LORD;
  They will praise Your holy name.
For You are great and perform wonderful deeds.
You alone are God.
Teach us Your ways, O LORD,
  that we may live according to Your truth!
Grant us purity of heart, so that we may honor You.
With all our heart we will praise You, O LORD our God.

You are our God.
You are so good.
You are so ready to forgive.
You are great and perform wonderful deeds.
You alone are God.

We will give glory to Your name forever,
  for Your love for us is very great.
You have rescued us from the depths of death.
O God, arrogant men oppose us;
  At times, we feel like they want to kill us.
You mean nothing to them.

But You, O LORD, are a God of compassion and mercy,
  slow to get angry
  and filled with unfailing love and faithfulness.
Look down and have mercy on us.
Give Your strength to us, Your servants;
  Save us, because we serve You just as our mothers did.
Send us a sign of Your favor.
Then those who hate us will be put to shame,
  because You, O LORD, have helped and comforted us.

Your love for us is very great.
You have rescued us.
You are a God of compassion and mercy.
You are slow to get angry.
You are filled with unfailing love and faithfulness.

87

On the holy mountain stands the city You founded.
You love the city of Jerusalem
  more than any other city in Israel.
And what glorious things are said of her—Your city.

You will count Egypt and Babylon
  among those who know You—
  also Philistia and Tyre, and even distant Ethiopia.
They have all become citizens of Jerusalem!
Regarding Jerusalem it will be said,
  "Everyone enjoys the rights of citizenship there."
And You will personally bless this city.
When You register the nations, You will say,
  "They have all become citizens of Jerusalem."

The people will play flutes and sing,
  "All our springs of joy are in You."

You love Jerusalem.
You are the source of all joy.

88

LORD, You are the God of our salvation.
We cry to You by day. We come to You at night.
Hear our prayer. Listen to our cry.
For our lives are full of troubles, and death draws near.
We are as good as dead, like strong men with no strength left.
Forsaken among the dead, like corpses in graves.
We feel forgotten, cut off from Your care.
You have thrown us into the lowest pit,
in dark places, in the depths.
Your wrath has rested upon us,
with wave after wave You have engulfed us.

You have driven our friends away
by making us repulsive to them.
We are in a trap with no way of escape.
Our eyes are blinded by our tears.
Each day we beg for Your help, O LORD;
We lift our hands to You for mercy.
Are Your wonderful deeds of any use to the dead?
Do the dead rise up and praise You?

Can those in the grave declare Your unfailing love?
Can they proclaim Your faithfulness
in the place of destruction?
Can the darkness speak of Your wonderful deeds?
Can anyone in the land of forgetfulness
talk about Your righteousness?
O LORD, we cry out to You.
We will keep on pleading day by day.

You are the God of our salvation.

O Lord, why does it feel like You are rejecting us?
Why does it seem as though
You have turned Your face from us?

We feel like we have been sick and close to death
since our youth.
We stand helpless and desperate before Your terrors.
Your fierce anger has overwhelmed us.
Your terrors have paralyzed us.
They swirl around us like floodwaters all day long.
They have engulfed us completely.

We feel like You have taken away our companions
and loved ones and made darkness our closest friend.

You are the God of our salvation.

89

We will sing of Your unfailing love forever!
Young and old will hear of Your faithfulness.
Your unfailing love will last forever.
Your faithfulness is as enduring as the heavens.
You have said:

"I have made a covenant with David, My chosen servant.
I have sworn this oath to him:
'I will establish your descendants as kings forever;
They will sit on your throne from now until eternity.'"

All heaven will praise Your great wonders, Lord;
Myriads of angels will praise You for Your faithfulness.
For who in all of heaven can compare with You?
What mightiest angel is anything like You, Lord?
The highest angelic powers stand in awe of You.
You are far more awesome
than all who surround Your throne.

O Lord God of Heaven's Armies!
Where is there anyone as mighty as You, O Lord?
You are entirely faithful.
You rule the oceans.
You subdue their storm-tossed waves.
You crushed the great sea monster.
You scattered Your enemies with Your mighty arm.

Your unfailing love will last forever.
You are entirely faithful.

The heavens are Yours, and the earth is Yours;
  Everything in the world is Yours—You created it all.
You created north and south.
Mount Tabor and Mount Hermon praise Your name.
Powerful is Your arm!
Strong is Your hand!
Your right hand is lifted high in glorious strength.

Righteousness and justice are the foundation of Your throne.
Lovingkindness and truth go before You.
Happy are those who hear the joyful call to worship,
  for they will walk in the light of Your presence, LORD.
They rejoice all day long in Your wonderful reputation.
They exult in Your righteousness.
You are their glorious strength.
It pleases You to make us strong.
Yes, our protection comes from You, LORD,
  and You, the Holy One of Israel, have given us our King.

Long ago You spoke in a vision
  to Your faithful people, saying:

"I have raised up a warrior. I have selected him
  from the common people to be king.
I have found My servant David.
I have anointed him with My holy oil.
I will steady him with My hand;
  With My powerful arm I will make him strong.
His enemies will not defeat him,
  nor will the wicked overpower him.
I will beat down his adversaries before him
  and destroy those who hate him.

You created everything.
You make us strong.
You protect us.

My faithfulness and unfailing love will be with him,
  and by My authority he will grow in power.
I will extend his rule over the sea,
  his dominion over the rivers.
And he will call out to Me, 'You are my Father,
  my God, and the Rock of my salvation.'
I will make him, My firstborn son,
  the mightiest king on earth.
I will love him and be kind to him forever;
  My covenant with him will never end.
I will preserve an heir for him;
  His throne will be as endless as the days of heaven.

But if his descendants forsake My instructions
  and fail to obey My regulations,
  if they do not obey My decrees
  and fail to keep My commands,
  then I will punish their sin with the rod
  and their disobedience with beating.
But I will never stop loving him
  nor fail to keep My promise to him.
No, I will not break My covenant;
  I will not take back a single word I said.
I have sworn an oath to David,
  and in My holiness I cannot lie.
His dynasty will go on forever;
  His kingdom will endure as the sun.
It will be as eternal as the moon,
  My faithful witness in the sky."

You cannot lie.

But then You rejected him and cast him off.
You were angry with Your anointed king.
You renounced Your covenant with him;
  You threw his crown in the dust.
You broke down the walls protecting him
  and ruined every fort defending him.
Everyone who came along robbed him,
  and he became a joke to his neighbors.
You strengthened his enemies and made them all rejoice.
You made his sword useless and refused to help him in battle.
You ended his splendor and overturned his throne.
You made him old before his time
  and publicly disgraced him.

O Lord, when we feel abandoned by You, we ask:
  "How long will this go on?
  Will You hide Yourself forever?
  How long will Your anger burn like fire?"
Remember how short our lives are,
  how empty and futile is this human existence!
No one can live forever; All will die.
No one can escape the power of the grave.

Lord, where is Your unfailing love?
You promised it to David with a faithful pledge.
Consider, Lord, how Your servants are disgraced!
We carry in our hearts the insults of so many people.
Your enemies have mocked us, O Lord;
  And they mock Your anointed.
We will praise You forever, Lord.
Amen and amen!

You promise Your unfailing love.

90

Lord, through all the generations You have been man's home!
Before the mountains were born,
before You gave birth to the earth and the world,
from beginning to end, You are God.

You turn people back to dust, saying,
"Return to dust, you mortals!"
For You, a thousand years are as a passing day,
as brief as a few night hours.
You sweep people away like dreams that disappear.
They are like grass that springs up in the morning.
In the morning it blooms and flourishes,
but by evening it is dry and withered.

We wither beneath Your anger;
We are overwhelmed by Your fury.
You spread out our sins before You—
our secret sins—and You see them all.
We live our lives beneath Your wrath,
ending our years with a groan.
Seventy years are given to us! Maybe eighty.
But even the best years are filled with pain and trouble;
Soon they disappear, and we will fly away.
Who can comprehend the power of Your anger?
Your wrath is as awesome as the fear You deserve.
Teach us to realize the brevity of life,
so that we may grow in wisdom.

You are God.
You see all our secret sins.

O LORD, come back to us!
How long will You delay?
Take pity on us, Your servants.

Satisfy us each morning with Your unfailing love,
so we may sing for joy to the end of our lives.
Give us gladness in proportion to our former misery.
Replace the evil years with good.
Let us, Your servants, see You work again;
Let our children see Your glory.

O Lord, our God, show us Your approval
and make our efforts successful.
Yes, make our efforts successful!

Your love is unfailing.

91

You tell us that when we abide in Your shelter,
  Almighty God, we will find rest in Your shadow.
This we declare about You, LORD:
  You alone are our refuge, our place of safety;
  You are our God, and we trust You.
For You will rescue us from every trap
  and protect us from deadly disease.
You will cover us with Your feathers.
You will shelter us with Your wings.
Your faithful promises are our armor and protection.

We will not be afraid of the terrors of the night,
  nor the arrow that flies in the day.
We will not dread the disease that stalks in darkness,
  nor the disaster that strikes at midday.
Though a thousand fall at our side,
  though ten thousand are dying around us,
  we know that these evils will not touch us.
We will just open our eyes
  and see how the wicked are punished.
If we make You our refuge, if we make You our shelter,
  no evil will conquer us;
  No plague will come near our homes.

For You will give Your angels charge concerning us,
  to guard us in all our ways.
They will bear us up in their hands,
  that we do not strike our feet against a stone.
We will tread upon the lion and cobra;
  The young lion and the serpent we will trample down.

You alone are our refuge, our place of safety.
You hear us when we call.

You say that, because we love You, You will rescue us
and protect us, because we trust in Your name.
You promise that, when we call on You, You will answer us
and be with us in trouble and will rescue and honor us.
You will reward us with long life
and give us Your salvation.

You are our salvation.

92

It is good to give thanks to You, Lord,
to sing praises to You, the Most High.
It is good to proclaim Your unfailing love in the morning,
Your faithfulness in the evening,
accompanied by a ten-stringed instrument,
a harp, and the melody of a lyre.

You thrill us, Lord, with all You have done for us!
We sing for joy because of what You have done.
O Lord, what great works You do!
And how deep are Your thoughts.
Senseless people have no knowledge,
and only fools would not understand this:
That when the wicked sprouted up like grass
and evildoers flourished,
it was only that they might be destroyed forevermore.

But You, O Lord, will be exalted forever.
Your enemies, Lord, will surely perish;
All evildoers will be scattered.
But You have made us as strong as wild oxen.
You have anointed us with the finest oil.
Our eyes have seen the downfall of our enemies;
Our ears have heard the defeat of our wicked opponents.

Your love is unfailing.
You are forever faithful.
You do great works.

You assure us that, as righteous people,
we will flourish like palm trees.
We will grow strong like cedars in Lebanon.
Planted in Your house, we will flourish in Your courts.
Even in old age, we will still produce fruit
and remain vital and green.
We will declare, "The Lord is just! He is our rock!
There is no evil in Him!"

You are just.
You are our rock.

93

You, Lord, are king! You are robed in majesty.
Indeed, You are robed in majesty and armed with strength.
The world stands firm and cannot be shaken.

Your throne, O Lord, is established from of old;
  You are from everlasting.
The floods have risen up, O Lord.
The floods have roared like thunder;
  The floods have lifted their pounding waves.
But mightier than the violent raging of the seas,
  mightier than the breakers on the shore—
  You are mightier than these!
Your royal laws cannot be changed.
Your reign, O Lord, is holy forever and ever.

You are King.
You are robed in majesty.
You are eternal.
You are mightier than the violent raging of the seas.
You are mightier than the breakers on the shore.
You are holy.

94

O Lord, God of vengeance,
  O God of vengeance, let Your glorious justice shine forth!
Rise up, O Judge of the earth.
Give the proud what they deserve.
How long, O Lord?
How long will the wicked be allowed to gloat?
How long will they speak with arrogance?
How long will these evil people boast?
They crush Your people, Lord,
  hurting those You claim as Your own.
They kill widows and foreigners and murder orphans.
"The Lord isn't looking," they say,
  "and besides, the God of Israel doesn't care."

We want to say, "Think again, you fools!
  When will you finally catch on?
  Is He deaf—the One who made your ears?
  Is He blind—the One who formed your eyes?
  He punishes the nations—won't He also punish you?
  He knows everything—
    doesn't He also know what you are doing?"

You know people's thoughts; You know they are worthless!
Joyful are those You discipline, Lord,
  those You teach with Your instructions.
You give them relief from troubled times
  until a pit is dug to capture the wicked.
You will not reject Your people;
  You will not abandon Your special possession.
Judgment will again be founded on justice,
  and those with virtuous hearts will pursue it.

You know people's thoughts.
You will not abandon Your people.

Who will protect us from the wicked?
Who will stand up for us against evildoers?
Unless You had helped us,
we would soon have settled in the silence of the grave.
We cried out, "We are slipping!"
But Your unfailing love, O LORD, supported us.
When doubts filled our minds,
Your comfort gave us renewed hope and cheer.
Can unjust leaders claim that You are on their side—
leaders whose decrees permit injustice?

They gang up against the righteous
and condemn the innocent to death.
But You are our fortress;
You are the mighty rock where we hide.
You will turn the sins of evil people back on them.
You will destroy them for their sins.
You, LORD, our God, will destroy them.

You are our fortress.
You are the mighty rock.
You will destroy evil people.

95

We will sing for joy to You, LORD.
We will shout joyfully to the Rock of our salvation.
We will come before Your presence with thanksgiving.
We will shout joyfully to You with psalms.
For You, LORD, are a great God
  and a great King above all gods.
In Your hand are the depths of the earth,
  and the peaks of the mountains are Yours also.
The sea is Yours, for it was You who made it,
  and Your hands formed the dry land.
We will worship and bow down.
We will kneel before You, LORD, our Maker.
For You are our God, and we are Yours.
You watch over us, as part of the flock under Your care.
Enable us to hear Your voice, LORD.
You have commanded us to not harden our hearts,
  as Israel did at Meribah,
  as they did at Massah in the wilderness,
  when our forefathers tested You and tried You,
  though they had seen Your work.
For forty years You were angry with them
  and said that they were a people
  whose hearts turn away from You.
They refused to do what You told them.
Therefore, in Your anger, You swore that
  they would never enter Your place of rest.
Please let that never be our fate, LORD.

You are a great God.
You are a great King, above all gods.
You made the sea and the land.
You made us and watch over us.
You speak to us.
You welcome us into Your place of rest.

96

We will sing a new song to You, LORD!
May the whole earth sing to You!
We will sing to You, LORD and praise Your name.
Each day we will proclaim the good news that You save.
We will publish Your glorious deeds among the nations.
We will tell everyone about the amazing things You do.
Great are You LORD! You are most worthy of praise!
You are to be feared above all gods.
The gods of other nations are mere idols,
but You made the heavens!
Honor and majesty surround You;
Strength and beauty fill Your sanctuary.

The nations of the world will recognize You, LORD;
They will recognize that You are glorious and strong.
We will give You the glory You deserve.
We will bring our offering and come into Your courts.
We will worship You, LORD, in all Your holy splendor.
May all the earth tremble before You.
We will tell all the nations that You reign,
that the world stands firm and cannot be shaken,
and that You will judge all peoples fairly.

You save.
You are great.
You are worthy of praise.
You are to be feared.
You made the heavens.
You deserve all glory.
You reign.
You will judge everyone fairly.

May the heavens be glad, and the earth rejoice!
May the sea and everything in it shout Your praise!
May the fields and their crops burst out with joy!
May the trees of the forest sing for joy before You,
  for You are coming!
You are coming to judge the earth.
You will judge the world with justice
  and the nations with Your truth.

You are coming to judge the earth.

97

You reign, may the earth be glad;
May the distant shores rejoice.
Clouds and thick darkness surround You;
Righteousness and justice
are the foundation of Your throne.
Fire goes before You and consumes Your foes on every side.
Your lightning lights up the world;
The earth sees and trembles.
The mountains melt like wax before You,
before You, the LORD of all the earth.
The heavens proclaim Your righteousness,
and all peoples see Your glory.

Those who worship idols are disgraced—
all who brag about their worthless gods—
for every god must bow to You.
Jerusalem has heard and rejoiced,
and all the towns of Judah are glad
because of Your justice, O LORD!
For You, O LORD, are supreme over all the earth;
You are exalted far above all gods.
We love You LORD. Teach us to hate evil.
You protect the lives of Your faithful followers
and rescue them from the power of the wicked.
Light shines on the godly,
and joy on those whose hearts are right.
May all who are godly rejoice in You, LORD,
and praise Your holy name!

You reign.
You are supreme over all the earth.
You protect the lives of Your faithful followers.

98

We will sing a new song to You, Lord,
for You have done wonderful things.
Your right hand and Your holy arm
have gained the victory for You.
You have made known Your salvation.
You have revealed Your righteousness to every nation.
You have remembered Your promise to love
and be faithful to Israel.
The ends of the earth have seen Your salvation.

May the whole earth shout joyfully to You, Lord
and break out in praise and sing for joy
and sing Your praise with the harp,
with the harp and the sound of melody,
and with trumpets and the sound of the horn,
making a joyful symphony before You, Lord, our King!

May the sea and everything in it shout Your praise!
May the earth and all living things join in.
May the rivers clap their hands in glee!
May the hills sing out their songs of joy
before You, Lord,
for You are coming to judge the earth.
You will judge the world with justice,
and the nations with fairness.

You have done wonderful things.
You have made known Your salvation.
You have revealed Your righteousness to every nation.
You are coming to judge the world
with justice and fairness.

99

You, LORD, are king!
Make the nations tremble!
You sit on Your throne between the cherubim.
Make the whole earth quake!
You, LORD, sit in majesty in Jerusalem,
  exalted above all the nations.
Let them praise Your great and awesome name.
Your name is holy!

Mighty King, lover of justice,
  You have established fairness.
You have acted with justice
  and righteousness throughout Israel.
We will exalt You, LORD, our God!
We will bow low before Your feet, for You are holy!
Moses and Aaron were among Your priests.
Samuel also called on Your name.

They cried to You, LORD, for help,
  and You answered them.
You spoke to Israel from the pillar of cloud,
  and they followed the laws and decrees You gave them.
O LORD, our God, You answered them.
You were a forgiving God to them,
  but You punished them when they went wrong.

We will exalt You, LORD, our God!
  and worship at Your holy mountain in Jerusalem,
  for You, LORD, our God, are holy!

You are our king.
Your name is holy.
You are holy.

100

We will shout joyfully to You, LORD.
We will serve You with gladness.

We will come before You with joyful singing.
We know that You Yourself are God.

It is You who has made us, and not we ourselves.
We are Yours, sheep of Your pasture.

We will enter Your gates with thanksgiving
and Your courts with praise.

We will give thanks to You and bless Your name.
For You are good.

Your lovingkindness is everlasting
and Your faithfulness is to all generations.

You are God.
You made us.
You are good.
Your love and Your faithfulness endure forever.

101

We will sing of Your love and justice, Lord.
We will praise You with songs.
We will be careful to live blameless lives.

When will You come to help us?
We will lead lives of integrity in our own homes.
We will set no worthless thing before our eyes.
We hate the work of those who fall away.
It shall not fasten its grip on us.
Perverse hearts shall depart from us;
We will know no evil.
We will not tolerate people who slander their neighbors.
We will not endure conceit and pride.

We will search for faithful people to be our companions.
Only those who are above reproach will minister to us.
We will not allow deceivers to serve in our houses,
and liars will not stay in our presence.

Lord, give us hearts that hate wickedness as David did,
as he each day sought to destroy all the wicked of the land,
and to cut them off from Your city.

You deserve our praise and our full devotion.

102

Lord, hear our prayer! Listen to our plea!
Don't turn away from us in our time of distress.
Bend down to listen,
 and answer us quickly when we call to You.
For our days disappear like smoke,
 and our bones burn like red-hot coals.
Our hearts are sick, withered like grass,
 and we have lost our appetites.
Because of our groaning, we are reduced to skin and bones.
We are like owls in the desert,
 like little owls in a far-off wilderness.
We lie awake, lonely as a solitary bird on the roof.
Our enemies taunt us day after day. They mock and curse us.
We feel like David, who ate ashes for food
 and whose tears ran down into his drink
 because of Your anger and wrath.
We feel like You have picked us up and thrown us out.
Our lives pass as swiftly as the evening shadows.
We are withering away like grass.

But You, O Lord, will sit on Your throne forever.
Your fame will endure to every generation.
You will arise and have mercy on Jerusalem—
 for now is the time to be gracious to her,
 now is the time You promised to help.
For Your people love every stone in her walls
 and cherish even the dust in her streets.
Then the nations will tremble before You, Lord.
The kings of the earth will tremble before Your glory.

You will sit on Your throne forever.

For You will rebuild Jerusalem.
You will appear in Your glory.
You will listen to the prayers of the destitute.
You will not reject their pleas.

Let this be recorded for future generations,
  so that a people not yet born will praise You, LORD.
For You looked down from Your heavenly sanctuary.
You looked down to earth from heaven
  to hear the groans of the prisoners,
  to release those condemned to die.
And so Your fame will be celebrated in Zion,
  Your praises in Jerusalem,
  when multitudes gather together
  and kingdoms come to worship You, LORD.

You broke our strength in midlife, cutting short our days.
But we cried to You:

  O God, who lives forever,
    don't take our lives while we are so young!
  Long ago You laid the foundation of the earth
    and made the heavens with Your hands.
  They will perish, but You remain forever;
    They will wear out like old clothing.
  You will change them like a garment and discard them.
  But You are always the same; You will live forever.
  The children of Your people will live in security.
  Their children's children will thrive in Your presence.

You will appear in Your glory.
You live forever.
You laid the foundation of the earth.

103

Let all that we are praise You, Lord;
And all that is within us, we will praise Your holy name.
Let all that we are praise You, Lord;
And may we never forget all that You have done
and do for us.
You forgive all our sins and heal all our diseases.
You redeem us from death
and crown us with love and compassion.
You fill our lives with good things,
so that our youth is renewed like the eagle.

You perform righteous deeds
and judgments for all who are oppressed.
You made known Your ways to Moses,
Your acts to the sons of Israel.
You are compassionate and gracious,
Slow to anger and abounding in lovingkindness.
You will not always strive with us,
nor will You keep Your anger forever.
You have not dealt with us according to our sins,
nor rewarded us according to our iniquities.
For as high as the heavens are above the earth,
so great is Your lovingkindness
toward those who fear You.
As far as the east is from the west,
so far have You removed our transgressions from us.

You forgive all our sins.
You fill our lives with good things.
You are compassionate and gracious.
You are slow to anger.
You remove our transgressions from us.

Just as a father has compassion on his children,
so You have compassion on those who fear You.
For You know how weak we are;
You remember we are only dust.
As for us, our days are like grass;
Like wildflowers, we bloom and then die.
The wind blows, and we are gone,
as though we had never been here.
But Your love remains forever with those who fear You.
Your salvation extends to the children's children
of those who keep Your covenant,
of those who obey Your commandments.

You have made the heavens Your throne;
And, from there, You rule over everything.
May all of Your angels praise You, LORD;
Those mighty in strength,
who perform Your word, obeying the voice of Your word!
May all of Your armies of angels praise You, LORD;
Those who serve You and do Your will.
May all that You have created, praise You, LORD,
everything in Your kingdom.
Let all that we are praise You, LORD.

You rule over everything.

104

Let all that we are praise You, Lord.
O Lord our God, how great You are!
You are robed with honor and majesty.
You are dressed in a robe of light.
You stretch out the starry curtain of the heavens.
You lay out the rafters of Your home in the rain clouds.
You make the clouds Your chariot.
You ride upon the wings of the wind.
The winds are Your messengers;
  Flames of fire are Your servants.

You placed the world on its foundation
  so it would never be moved.
You clothed the earth with floods of water,
  water that covered even the mountains.
At Your command, the water fled;
  At the sound of Your thunder, it hurried away.
Mountains rose and valleys sank to the levels You decreed.
Then You set a firm boundary for the seas,
  so they would never again cover the earth.

You make springs pour water into the ravines,
  so streams gush down from the mountains.
They provide water for all the animals,
  and the wild donkeys quench their thirst.
The birds nest beside the streams
  and sing among the branches of the trees.

You are great.
You created everything.

You send rain on the mountains from Your heavenly home,
    and You fill the earth with the fruit of Your labor.
You cause grass to grow for the livestock
    and plants for people to use.
You allow them to produce food from the earth—
    wine to make them glad,
    olive oil to soothe their skin,
    and bread to give them strength.
Your trees are well cared for—
    the cedars of Lebanon that You planted.

There, the birds make their nests,
    and the storks make their homes in the cypresses.
High in the mountains live the wild goats,
    and the rocks form a refuge for the hyraxes.
You made the moon to mark the seasons,
    and the sun knows when to set.
You send the darkness, and it becomes night,
    when all the forest animals prowl about.
Then the young lions roar for their prey,
    stalking the food You provided.
At dawn they slink back into their dens to rest.
Then people go off to their work,
    where they labor until evening.

O LORD, what a variety of things You have made!
In wisdom, You have made them all.
The earth is full of Your creatures.
Here is the ocean, vast and wide,
    teeming with life of every kind, both large and small.

You maintain everything.

We see the ships sailing along, and Leviathan,
 which You made to play in the sea.
They all depend on You to give them food as they need it.
When You supply it, they gather it.
You open Your hand to feed them,
 and they are richly satisfied.
But if You turn away from them, they panic.
When You take away their breath,
 they die and turn again to dust.
When You give them Your breath, life is created,
 and You renew the face of the earth.

May Your glory continue forever!
You take pleasure in all You have made!
The earth trembles at Your glance;
 The mountains smoke at Your touch.
We will sing to You, LORD, as long as we live.
We will praise You, our God, to our last breath!
May all our thoughts be pleasing to You,
 for we rejoice in You, LORD.
Let all sinners vanish from the face of the earth;
 Let the wicked disappear forever.
Let all that we are praise You, LORD.
We Praise You, LORD!

You take pleasure in all You have made.

105

We give thanks to You, Lord, and proclaim Your greatness.
We will do our part to let the whole world know
  what You have done.
We will sing to You; Yes, sing Your praises.
We will tell everyone about Your wonderful deeds.
We will exult in Your holy name
  and rejoice as we worship You, Lord.
We will search for You, Lord, and for Your strength.
We will continually seek You.
As You commanded the children of Your servant Abraham,
  (the descendants of Jacob, Your chosen ones),
  we will remember the wonders You have performed,
  Your miracles, and the rulings You have given.
You are the Lord our God.
Your justice is seen throughout the land.
You always stand by Your covenant—
  the commitment You made to a thousand generations.
This is the covenant You made with Abraham
  and the oath You swore to Isaac.
You confirmed it to Jacob as a decree,
  and to the people of Israel as a never-ending covenant:
  "I will give you the land of Canaan
  as your special possession."
You said this when they were few in number,
  a tiny group of strangers in Canaan.
They wandered from nation to nation,
  from one kingdom to another.
Yet You did not let anyone oppress them.
You warned kings on their behalf:
  "Do not touch My chosen people,
  and do not hurt My prophets."

You are great.
You stand by Your covenant.

You called for a famine on the land of Canaan,
  cutting off its food supply.
Then You sent someone to Egypt ahead of them—
  Joseph, who was sold as a slave.
They bruised his feet with fetters
  and placed his neck in an iron collar.
Until the time came to fulfill his dreams,
  You tested Joseph's character.
Then Pharaoh sent for him and set him free;
  The ruler of the nation opened his prison door.
Joseph was put in charge of all the king's household;
  He became ruler over all the king's possessions.
He could instruct the king's aides as he pleased
  and teach the king's advisers.
Then Israel arrived in Egypt;
  Jacob lived as a foreigner in the land of Ham.
And You multiplied the people of Israel
  until they became too mighty for their enemies.

Then You turned the Egyptians against the Israelites,
  and they plotted against Your servants.
But You sent Your servant Moses, along with Aaron,
  whom You had chosen.
They performed miraculous signs among the Egyptians,
  and wonders in the land of Ham.
You blanketed Egypt in darkness,
  for they had defied Your commands to let Your people go.
You turned their water into blood, poisoning all the fish.
Then frogs overran the land
  and even invaded the king's bedrooms.
When You spoke, flies descended on the Egyptians,
  and gnats swarmed across Egypt.
You sent them hail instead of rain,
  and lightning flashed over the land.

You orchestrate everything.

You ruined their grapevines and fig trees
and shattered all the trees.
You spoke, and hordes of locusts came—
young locusts beyond number.
They ate up everything green in the land,
destroying all the crops in their fields.
Then You killed the oldest son in each Egyptian home,
the pride and joy of each family.

You brought Your people out of Egypt,
loaded with silver and gold;
And not one among the tribes of Israel even stumbled.
Egypt was glad when they were gone,
for they feared them greatly.
You spread a cloud above them as a covering
and gave them a great fire to light the darkness.
They asked for meat, and You sent them quail.
You satisfied their hunger with manna—bread from heaven.
You split open a rock, and water gushed out
to form a river through the dry wasteland.
For You remembered Your sacred promise
to Your servant Abraham.
So You brought Your people out of Egypt with joy,
Your chosen ones with rejoicing.
You gave Your people the lands of pagan nations,
and they harvested crops that others had planted.
All this happened so they would follow Your decrees
and obey Your instructions.
We praise You, Lord!

You brought Your people out of Egypt.
You satisfied their hunger.

106

We praise You, LORD!
We give thanks to You, for You are good!
Your faithful love endures forever.
Who can list Your glorious miracles?
Who can ever praise You enough?
You tell us that there is joy for us if we deal justly with others
and always do what is right.

Remember us, LORD, when You show favor to Your people;
Come near and rescue us.
Let us share in the prosperity of Your chosen ones.
Let us rejoice in the joy of Your people.
Let us praise You with those who are Your heritage.

Like all those before us, we have sinned.
We have done wrong! We have acted wickedly!
Your people in Egypt were not impressed
by Your miraculous deeds.
They soon forgot Your many acts of kindness to them.
Instead, they rebelled against You at the Red Sea.
Even so, You saved them—to defend the honor of Your name
and to demonstrate Your mighty power.
You commanded the Red Sea to dry up.
You led Israel across the sea as if it were a desert.
So You rescued them from their enemies
and redeemed them from their foes.
Then the water returned and covered their enemies;
Not one of them survived.
Then Your people believed Your promises.
Then they sang Your praise.

You are good.

Yet how quickly they forgot what You had done!
They wouldn't wait for Your counsel!
In the wilderness their desires ran wild,
testing Your patience in that dry wasteland.
So You gave them what they asked for,
but You sent a plague along with it.

The people in the camp were jealous of Moses
and envious of Aaron, Your holy priest.
Because of this, the earth opened up;
It swallowed Dathan and buried Abiram
and the other rebels.
Fire fell upon their followers; A flame consumed the wicked.

The people made a calf at Mount Sinai;
They bowed before an image made of gold.
They traded You, their glorious God,
for a statue of a grass-eating bull.
They forgot You, their savior,
who had done such great things in Egypt—
such wonderful things in the land of Ham,
such awesome deeds at the Red Sea.
So You declared You would destroy them.
But Moses, Your chosen one,
stepped between You and the people.
He begged You to turn from Your anger
and not destroy them.
The people refused to enter the pleasant land,
for they wouldn't believe Your promise to care for them.
Instead, they grumbled in their tents and refused to obey You.
Therefore, You solemnly swore
that You would kill them in the wilderness,
that You would scatter their descendants
among the nations, exiling them to distant lands.

You are so patient.

Then they joined in the worship of Baal at Peor;
  They even ate sacrifices offered to the dead!
They angered You with all these things,
  so a plague broke out among them.
But Phinehas had the courage to intervene,
  and the plague was stopped.
So he has been regarded as a righteous man
  ever since that time.
At Meribah, too, they angered You, LORD,
  causing Moses serious trouble.
They made Moses angry, and he spoke foolishly.

Israel failed to destroy the nations in the land,
  as You had commanded them.
Instead, they mingled among the pagans
  and adopted their evil customs.
They worshiped their idols, which led to their downfall.
They even sacrificed their sons
  and their daughters to the demons.
They shed innocent blood,
  the blood of their sons and daughters.
By sacrificing them to the idols of Canaan,
  they polluted the land with murder.
They defiled themselves by their evil deeds,
  and their love of idols was adultery in Your sight.

That is why Your anger burned against Your people,
  and You abhorred Your own special possession.
You handed them over to pagan nations,
  and they were ruled by those who hated them.
Their enemies crushed them
  and brought them under their cruel power.

You get angry when we turn from You.

Again and again You rescued them,
but they chose to rebel against You,
and they were finally destroyed by their sin.
Even so, You pitied them in their distress
and listened to their cries.
You remembered Your covenant with them
and relented because of Your unfailing love.
You even caused their captors to treat them with kindness.

Save us, O Lord our God!
Gather us back from among the nations,
so we can thank Your holy name
and rejoice and praise You.
We praise You, Lord, God of Israel,
who lives from everlasting to everlasting!
Let all the people say, "Amen!"
We praise You, Lord!

Your love is unfailing.

107

We give thanks to You, Lord, for You are good!
Your faithful love endures forever.
You have redeemed us. So, we will speak out!
We will tell others that You have redeemed us
  from our enemies.
For You have gathered the exiles from many lands,
  from east and west, from north and south.
Some wandered in the wilderness, lost and homeless.
Hungry and thirsty, they nearly died.
"Lord, help!" they cried in their trouble,
  and You rescued them from their distress.
You led them straight to safety,
  to a city where they could live.
We will praise You, Lord, for Your great love
  and for the wonderful things You have done.
For You satisfy the thirsty soul
  and fill the hungry with good things.

Some sat in darkness and deepest gloom,
  imprisoned in iron chains of misery.
They rebelled against Your words, scorning Your counsel.
That is why You broke them with hard labor;
  They fell, and no one was there to help them.
"Lord, help!" they cried in their trouble,
  and You saved them from their distress.
You led them from the darkness and deepest gloom;
  You snapped their chains.
We will praise You, Lord, for Your great love
  and for the wonderful things You have done.
For You broke down their prison gates of bronze;
  You cut apart their bars of iron.

You are good.
You satisfy the thirsty soul.

Some were fools; They rebelled and suffered for their sins.
They couldn't stand the thought of food,
  and they were knocking on death's door.
"LORD, help!" they cried in their trouble,
  and You saved them from their distress.
You sent out Your word and healed them,
  and saved them from their destruction.
We will praise You, LORD, for Your great love
  and for the wonderful things You have done.
We will offer sacrifices of thanksgiving
  and sing joyfully about Your glorious acts.

Some went off to sea in ships,
  doing business on the great waters.
They, too, observed Your power in action,
  Your impressive works on the deepest seas.
You spoke, and the winds rose, stirring up the waves.
Their ships were tossed to the heavens
  and plunged again to the depths;
  The sailors cringed in terror.
They reeled and staggered like drunkards
  and were at their wits' end.
"LORD, help!" they cried in their trouble,
  and You saved them from their distress.
You calmed the storm to a whisper and stilled the waves.
What a blessing was that stillness
  as You brought them safely into harbor!
We will praise You, LORD, for Your great love
  and for the wonderful things You have done.
We will exalt You publicly before the congregation
  and before the leaders of the nation.

You are so powerful.
Your love is great.
You have done wonderful things.

You change rivers into deserts
   and springs of water into dry, thirsty land.
You turn the fruitful land into salty wastelands,
   because of the wickedness of those who live there.
But You also turn deserts into pools of water,
   the dry land into springs of water.
You bring the hungry to settle there and to build their cities.
They sow their fields, plant their vineyards,
   and harvest their bumper crops.
How You bless them!
They raise large families there,
   and their herds of livestock increase.

When they decrease in number and become impoverished
   through oppression, trouble, and sorrow,
   You pour contempt on their princes,
   causing them to wander in trackless wastelands.
But You rescue the poor from trouble
   and increase their families like flocks of sheep.
The godly will see these things and be glad,
   while the wicked are struck silent.
LORD, give us wisdom, to take all this to heart
   and to consider Your faithful love.

You rescue the poor from trouble.

108

Our hearts are steadfast, O God.
We will sing. We will sing praises, even with our souls.
We will awaken the dawn with our song!
We will give thanks to You, O LORD, among the peoples,
  and we will sing praises to You among the nations.
For Your lovingkindness is great above the heavens,
  and Your truth reaches to the skies.
Be exalted, O God, above the heavens,
  and Your glory above all the earth.
Rescue us, Your beloved, LORD.
Answer us and save us with Your right hand.

You promised, in Your holiness,
  that You would divide up Shechem with joy
  and measure out the valley of Succoth.
You claimed Gilead and Manasseh as Yours.
You called Ephraim Your helmet
  and said that it would produce Your warriors,
You called Judah Your scepter
  and said that it would produce Your kings.
But Moab, You called Your washbowl
  and said that it would become Your servant,
You also said that You would wipe Your feet on Edom
  and shout in triumph over Philistia.

Your lovingkindness is great above the heavens.
Your truth reaches to the skies.

Will You bring us, LORD,
through our tough battles and into safety?
Will You bring us victory over our enemies?
O God, it sure feels like You have rejected us.
Won't You go with us into battle?
Oh, LORD, give us help against the adversary,
for all human help is useless.
With Your help, God, we know we will do mighty things,
for You will trample down our adversaries.

You will trample down our adversaries.

109

O God, whom we praise, don't be silent!
Should the wicked slander us and tell lies about us
  and surround us with hateful words
  and fight against us for no reason?
In return for our love, if they accuse us,
  though we devote ourselves to prayer;
  If they repay evil for good and hatred for our love;
  If they say:

"Get an evil person to turn against them.
Send an accuser to bring them to trial.
When their cases come up for judgment,
  let them be pronounced guilty.
Count their prayers as sins. Let their years be few;
  Let someone else take their positions.
May their children become parentless,
  and their spouses become widows and widowers.
May their children wander as beggars
  and be driven from their ruined homes.
May creditors seize their estates,
  and strangers take all they have earned.

Let no one be kind to them;
  Let no one pity their parentless children.
May all their offspring die.
May their family names be blotted out
  in the next generation.
May the LORD never forget the sins of their fathers.
May their mothers' sins never be erased from the record.
May the LORD always remember these sins,
  and may their names disappear from human memory.

You are worthy of praise.

For they refused all kindness to others;
They persecuted the poor and needy,
and they hounded the brokenhearted to death.

They loved to curse others; Now You curse them.
They never blessed others; Now don't You bless them.
Cursing is as natural to them as their clothing,
or the water they drink, or the rich food they eat.
Now may their curses return
and cling to them like clothing;
May they be tied around them like belts."

If You choose to apply these curses to our accusers
who speak evil of us, let such punishment
be exactly what is needed for them to turn to You.
But deal well with us, O Sovereign LORD,
for the sake of Your own reputation!

Rescue us because You are so faithful and good.
For we are poor and needy, and our hearts are full of pain.
We are fading like shadows at dusk;
We are brushed off like locusts.
Our knees are weak from fasting, and we are skin and bones.
If we become a joke to people everywhere;
If when they see us, they shake their heads in scorn.
Help us, O LORD our God!
Save us because of Your unfailing love.

Let them see that this is Your doing,
that You Yourself have done it, LORD.
Then let them curse us if they like, but You will bless us!
When they attack us, they will be disgraced!
But we, Your servants, will go right on rejoicing!

You are so faithful and good.

May our accusers be clothed with disgrace;
May their humiliation cover them like a cloak.
But we will give repeated thanks to You, LORD,
praising You to everyone.
For You stand beside the needy,
ready to save them from those who condemn them.

You stand beside the needy.
You stand ready to save.

110

God, You say to Jesus, our Lord:
"Sit in the place of honor at My right hand
until I humble Your enemies,
making them a footstool under Your feet."
You will extend His scepter from Jerusalem, saying:
"Rule in the midst of Your enemies."

When He goes to war, His people will serve Him willingly.
He will be arrayed in holy garments,
and His strength will be renewed each day
like the morning dew.

God, You have sworn and will not break Your vow:
"You are a priest forever in the order of Melchizedek."

He is at Your right hand.
He will strike down many kings when His anger erupts.
He will punish the nations and fill their lands with corpses.
He will shatter heads over the whole earth.
He will be refreshed from brooks along the way.
He will be victorious.

You give dominion to the King.

111

We praise You, Lord!

We will thank You with all our heart
as we meet with Your godly people.
How amazing are Your deeds, Lord!
All who delight in You should ponder them.
Everything You do reveals Your glory and majesty.
Your righteousness never fails.
You cause us to remember Your wonderful works.
How gracious and merciful are You, our Lord!
You give food to those who fear You;
You always remember Your covenant.
You have shown Your great power to Your people
by giving them the lands of other nations.
All You do is just and good,
and all Your commandments are trustworthy.
They are forever true,
to be obeyed faithfully and with integrity.
You have paid a full ransom for Your people.
You have guaranteed Your covenant with them forever.
What a holy, awe-inspiring name You have!
Fear of You, Lord, is the foundation of true wisdom.
All who obey Your commandments will grow in wisdom.

We will praise You forever!

Your deeds are amazing.
Your righteousness never fails.
You give food to those who fear You.
You always remember Your covenant.
You have paid our ransom in full.
Your name is holy and awe-inspiring.

112

We praise You, LORD!

Teach us to fear You, LORD,
and to delight in obeying Your commands.
You tell us that, if we do so:

- Our children will be successful;
- An entire generation of godly people will be blessed;
- Wealth and riches will be in our houses;
- Our righteousness will endure forever; and
- Light will arise in the darkness for us.

You tell us that, if we are gracious, merciful, and righteous;
lend money generously; and conduct our business fairly:

- It will go well with us;
- We will not be overcome by evil;
- We will be long remembered;
- We will not fear bad news;
- We will confidently trust You to care for us;
- We will be confident and fearless
  and be able to face our foes triumphantly;
- We will share freely
  and give generously to those in need;
- Our good deeds will be remembered forever; and
- We will have influence and honor.

The wicked will see this and be infuriated.
They will grind their teeth in anger;
They will slink away, their hopes thwarted.

You bless those who fear You
and walk in Your way.

113

We praise You, LORD!

Yes, we give You praise, as Your servants, LORD.
We praise Your name, LORD!
Blessed be Your name now and forever.
Everywhere—from east to west—
  we praise Your name, LORD.
For You are high above the nations;
  Your glory is higher than the heavens.

Who can be compared with You, LORD, our God,
  You who are enthroned on high?
You stoop to look down
  on heaven and on earth.
You lift the poor from the dust
  and the needy from the garbage dump.
You set them among princes,
  even the princes of Your own people!
You give the childless woman a family,
  making her a happy mother.

We praise You, LORD!

You are high above the nations.
Your glory is higher than the heavens.
You are beyond comparison.
You are enthroned on high.
You care for the poor.

114

When the Israelites escaped from Egypt—
when the family of Jacob left that foreign land—
the land of Judah became Your sanctuary,
and Israel became Your kingdom.

The Red Sea saw them coming and fled;
The water of the Jordan River turned away.
The mountains skipped like rams, the hills like lambs!

Had we been there, we likely would have mocked:

“What’s wrong, Red Sea,
that made you hurry out of their way?
What happened, Jordan River, that you turned away?
Why, mountains, did you skip like rams?
Why, hills, like lambs?”

At Your presence, Lord, the earth trembled,
at Your presence, O God of Jacob.
You turned the rock into a pool of water;
Yes, a spring of water flowed from solid rock.

Your presence causes the whole earth to tremble.

115

Not to us, O Lord, not to us,
but to Your name we give glory,
because of Your lovingkindness, because of Your truth.
Why should the nations say,
"Where, now, is their God?"

But You, our God, are in the heavens;
You do whatever You please.
Their idols are silver and gold,
the work of man's hands.

They have mouths, but they cannot speak.
They have eyes, but they cannot see.
They have ears, but they cannot hear.
They have noses, but they cannot smell.
They have hands, but they cannot feel.
They have feet, but they cannot walk.
They cannot make a sound with their throat.
Those who make them will become like them,
everyone who trusts in them.

As the psalmist pleaded with Israel to trust in You,
for You were their help and their shield,
give us the courage to trust in You.
As he pleaded with the house of Aaron to trust in You,
for You were their help and their shield,
give us the courage to trust in You.

You are worthy of all glory.

Give us the courage to fear You, O Lord,
and to trust in You.
You are our help and our shield.
You have been mindful of us; You will bless us.
You will bless the house of Israel.
You will bless the house of Aaron.
You will bless those who fear You,
the small together with the great.

Lord, give us increase, us and our children.
Bless us, O Lord, maker of heaven and earth.

The heavens are Your heavens,
but the earth You have given to the sons of men.
The dead do not praise You,
nor do any who go down into silence.
But as for us, we will bless You, Lord,
from this time forth and forever.

We praise You, Lord!

You are our help and our shield.
You will bless us.

116

We love You, Lord, because You hear our voices
  and our prayers for mercy.
Because You bend down to listen,
  we will call upon You as long as we live.
Even if death wraps its ropes around us
  or the terrors of the grave overtake us.
Even when we see only trouble and sorrow,
  we will call on Your name: "Please, Lord, save us!"

How kind You are! How good You are!
  So merciful are You, our God!
You protect those of childlike faith;
  We were facing death, and You saved us.
Let our souls be at rest again, for You have been good to us.

You have saved us from death,
  our eyes from tears, our feet from stumbling.
And so we walk in Your presence as we live here on earth!
We believed in You, so we said,
  "We are deeply troubled, Lord."
In our anxiety, we cried out to You,
  "These people are all liars!"

You hear us.
You are kind.
You are good.
You are merciful.
You protect those of childlike faith.
You have been good to us.
You have saved us from death.

What can we offer You, Lord
  for all You have done for us?
We will lift up the cup of salvation
  and praise Your name for saving us.
We will keep our promises to You, O Lord,
  in the presence of all Your people.
You care deeply when Your loved ones die.

O Lord, we are Your servants;
  Yes, we are Your servants, born into Your household;
  You have freed us from our chains.
We will offer You a sacrifice of thanksgiving
  and call on Your name.
We will fulfill our vows to You, O Lord,
  in the presence of all Your people—
  in Your house, O Lord.

We praise You Lord!

You have freed us from our chains.

117

May all the nations praise You, LORD.

May all the people of the earth praise You.

For Your unfailing love for us is powerful;
Your faithfulness endures forever.

We praise You, LORD!

Your unfailing love for us is powerful.
Your faithfulness endures forever.

118

We give thanks to You, Lord, for You are good!
Your faithful love endures forever.
Let all Israel repeat: "His faithful love endures forever."
Let Aaron's descendants, the priests, repeat:
"His faithful love endures forever."
Let all who fear You repeat:
"His faithful love endures forever."

In our distress, we pray to You, Lord,
and You answer us and set us free.
You are for us, so we will have no fear.
What can man do to us?
Yes, You are for us; You will help us.
We will look in triumph at those who hate us.
It is better to take refuge in You than to trust in people.
It is better to take refuge in You than to trust in princes.
Though hostile forces surrounded us,
in Your name, we overcame them.
Yes, they surrounded and attacked us,
but, in Your name, we overcame them.
They swarmed around us like bees;
They blazed against us like a crackling fire,
but, in Your name, we overcame them.
We were pushed hard, so that we were falling,
but You rescued us.
You are our strength and our song;
You have given us victory.

You are good.
Your love endures forever.
You answer us and set us free.
You are for us, and You will help us.
You are our strength and our song.
You give us victory.

Songs of joy and victory are sung in the camp of the godly.
Your strong right arm has done glorious things!
Your strong right arm is raised in triumph.
Your strong right arm has done glorious things!
We will not die;
Instead, we will live to tell what You have done.
You have punished us severely, but You did not let us die.
Open for us the gates where the righteous enter,
and we will go in and thank You.
These gates lead to Your presence, LORD,
and the godly enter there.
We thank You for answering our prayers
and giving us victory!

The stone that the builders rejected
has now become the cornerstone.
This is Your doing, and it is wonderful to see.
This is the day You have made.
We will rejoice and be glad in it.
Please, LORD, save us.
Please, LORD, give us success.

Bless those who come in Your name.
Bless those from Your house.
You are God, and You have given us light.
Please, LORD, receive with joy our sacrifices to You.

You are our God, and we will praise You!
You are our God, and we will exalt You!
We give thanks to You, for You are good!
Your faithful love endures forever.

You are the creator of each day.
You are our God.
You are good.
Your love endures forever.

119

You tell us we will be blessed, if our ways are blameless
  and if we follow Your instructions, LORD.
You tell us will be blessed, if we obey Your laws,
  if we search for You with all our heart,
  if we do not compromise with evil,
  and if we walk only in Your paths.
You have charged us to keep Your commandments carefully.
Oh, that our actions would consistently reflect Your decrees!
Then we will not be ashamed
  when we compare our lives with Your commands.
  As we learn Your righteous regulations,
  we will thank You by living as we should!
We will obey Your decrees. Please don't give up on us!

How can we keep our ways pure? By obeying Your word.
We have tried hard to find You—
  don't let us wander from Your commands.
We have hidden Your word in our hearts,
  that we might not sin against You.
We praise You, O LORD; Teach us Your decrees.
We have recited aloud all the regulations You have given us.
We have rejoiced in Your laws as much as in riches.
We will study Your commandments
  and reflect on Your ways.
We will delight in Your decrees and not forget Your word.

Your Word is good.

Be good to Your servants,
  that we may live and obey Your word.
Open our eyes to see
  the wonderful truths in Your instructions.
We are only foreigners in the land.
Don't hide Your commands from us!
We are always overwhelmed
  with a desire for Your regulations.
You rebuke the arrogant;
  Those who wander from Your commands are cursed.
Don't let them scorn and insult us,
  for we have obeyed Your laws.
Even princes sit and speak against us,
  but we will meditate on Your decrees.
Your laws please us; They give us wise advice.

We lie in the dust; Revive us by Your word.
We told You our plans, and You answered.
Now teach us Your decrees.
Help us understand the meaning of Your precepts,
  and we will meditate on Your wonderful deeds.
We weep with sorrow; Encourage us by Your word.
Keep us from lying to ourselves;
  Give us the privilege of knowing Your instructions.
We have chosen to be faithful;
  We have determined to live by Your regulations.
We cling to Your laws. LORD, don't let us be put to shame!
We will pursue Your commands,
  for You expand our understanding.

Your Word is good.

Teach us Your decrees, O Lord;
We will keep them to the end.
Give us understanding, that we may obey Your law
and keep it with all our heart.
Make us walk in the path of Your commands,
for that is where our happiness is found.
Give us an eagerness for Your laws
rather than a love for money!
Turn our eyes from worthless things,
and give us life through Your word.
Reassure us of Your promise, made to those who fear You.
Help us abandon our shameful ways;
For Your regulations are good.

We long to obey Your commandments!
Renew our lives with Your goodness.
Lord, give us Your unfailing love,
the salvation that You promised us.
Then we can answer those who taunt us,
for we trust in Your word.
Do not snatch Your word of truth from us,
for Your regulations are our only hope.
We will keep on obeying Your instructions forever and ever.
We will walk in freedom,
for we have devoted ourselves to Your commandments.
We will speak to kings about Your laws,
and we will not be ashamed.
How we delight in Your commands! How we love them!
We honor and love Your commands.
We meditate on Your decrees.

Your Word is good.

Remember Your promise to us; It is our only hope.
Your promise revives us; It comforts us in all our troubles.
The proud hold us in utter contempt,
  but we do not turn away from Your instructions.
We meditate on Your age-old regulations;
  O Lord, they comfort us.
We become furious with the wicked,
  because they reject Your instructions.
Your decrees have been the theme of our songs
  wherever we have lived.
We reflect at night on who You are, O Lord;
  Therefore, we obey Your instructions.
This is how we spend our lives:
  obeying Your commandments.

Lord, You are ours! We promise to obey Your words!
With all our heart we want Your blessings.
Be merciful as You promised.
We pondered the direction of our lives,
  and we turned to follow Your laws.
We will hurry, without delay, to obey Your commands.
Evil people try to drag us into sin,
  but we are firmly anchored to Your instructions.
We rise at midnight to thank You for Your just regulations.
We are friends to anyone who fears You—
  anyone who obeys Your commandments.
O Lord, Your unfailing love fills the earth;
  Teach us Your decrees.

Your Word is good.

You have done many good things for us, Lord,
just as You promised.
We believe in Your commands;
Now teach us good judgment and knowledge.
We used to wander off until You disciplined us;
But now we closely follow Your word.
You are good and do only good; Teach us Your decrees.
Arrogant people smear us with lies,
but in truth we obey Your commandments
with all our heart.
Their hearts are dull and stupid,
but we delight in Your instructions.
Our suffering was good for us,
for it taught us to pay attention to Your decrees.
Your instructions are more valuable to us
than millions in gold and silver.

You made us; You created us.
Now give us the sense to follow Your commands.
May all who fear You find in us a cause for joy,
for we have put our hope in Your word.
We know, O Lord, that Your regulations are fair;
You disciplined us because we needed it.
Now let Your unfailing love comfort us,
just as You promised us, Your servants.
Surround us with Your tender mercies so we may live,
for Your instructions are our delight.
May the arrogant, who lied about us, be ashamed;
Meanwhile, we will meditate on Your precepts.
Let us be united with all who fear You,
with those who know Your laws.
May we be blameless in keeping Your decrees;
Then we will never be ashamed.

Your Word is good.

We are worn out waiting for Your rescue,
   but we have put our hope in Your word.
Our eyes are straining to see Your promises come true.
When will You comfort us?
We are shriveled like a wineskin in the smoke,
   but we have not forgotten to obey Your decrees.
How long must we wait?
When will You punish those who persecute us?
These arrogant people who hate Your instructions
   have dug deep pits to trap us.
All Your commands are trustworthy.
Protect us from those who hunt us down without cause.
They almost finished us off,
   but we refused to abandon Your commandments.
In Your unfailing love, spare our lives;
   Then we can continue to obey Your laws.

Your eternal word, O Lord, stands firm in heaven.
Your faithfulness extends to every generation,
   as enduring as the earth You created.
Your regulations remain true to this day,
   for everything serves Your plans.
If Your instructions hadn't sustained us with joy,
   we would have died in our misery.
We will never forget Your commandments,
   for by them You give us life.
We are Yours; Rescue us!
For we have worked hard at obeying Your commandments.
Though the wicked hide along the way to kill us,
   we will quietly keep our minds on Your laws.
Even perfection has its limits,
   but Your commands have no limit.

Your Word is good.

Oh, how we love Your instructions!
We think about them all day long.
Your commands make us wiser than our enemies,
  for they are our constant guide.
Yes, we have more insight than our teachers,
  for we are always thinking of Your laws.
We are even wiser than our elders,
  for we have kept Your commandments.
We have refused to walk on any evil path,
  so that we may remain obedient to Your word.
We haven't turned away from Your regulations,
  for You have taught us well.
How sweet Your words taste to us;
  They are sweeter than honey.
Your commandments give us understanding;
  No wonder we hate every false way of life.

Your word is a lamp to guide our feet and a light for our path.
We've promised it once, and we'll promise it again:
  We will obey Your righteous regulations.
We have suffered much, O LORD;
  Restore our lives again as You promised.
LORD, accept our offerings of praise,
  and teach us Your regulations.
Our lives constantly hang in the balance,
  but we will not stop obeying Your instructions.
The wicked have set their traps for us,
  but we will not turn from Your commandments.
Your laws are our treasure; They are our hearts' delight.
We are determined to keep Your decrees to the very end.

Your Word is good.

We hate those with divided loyalties,
 but we love Your instructions.
You are our refuge and our shield;
 Your word is our source of hope.
We will say, "Get out of our lives, you evil-minded people,
 for we intend to obey the commands of our God."
LORD, sustain us as You promised, that we may live!
Do not let our hope be crushed.
Sustain us, and we will be rescued;
 Then we will meditate continually on Your decrees.
But You have rejected all who stray from Your decrees.
They are only fooling themselves.
You skim off the wicked of the earth like scum;
 No wonder we love to obey Your laws!
We tremble in fear of You;
 We stand in awe of Your regulations.

Don't leave us to the mercy of our enemies,
 for we have done what is just and right.
Please guarantee a blessing for us.
Don't let the arrogant oppress us!
Our eyes strain to see Your rescue,
 to see the truth of Your promise fulfilled.
We are Your servants; Deal with us in unfailing love,
 and teach us Your decrees.
Give discernment to us, Your servants;
 Then we will understand Your laws.
LORD, it is time for You to act,
 for these evil people have violated Your instructions.
Truly, we love Your commands more than gold,
 even the finest gold.
Each of Your commandments is right.
That is why we hate every false way.

Your Word is good.

Your laws are wonderful. No wonder we obey them!
The teaching of Your word gives light,
so even the simple can understand.
We pant with expectation, longing for Your commands.
Come and show us Your mercy,
as You do for all who love Your name.
Guide our steps by Your word,
so we will not be overcome by evil.
Ransom us from the oppression of evil people;
Then we can obey Your commandments.
Look upon us with love; Teach us Your decrees.
Rivers of tears gush from our eyes
because people disobey Your instructions.

O LORD, You are righteous, and Your regulations are fair.
Your laws are perfect and completely trustworthy.
We are overwhelmed with indignation,
for our enemies have disregarded Your words.
Your promises have been thoroughly tested;
That is why we love them so much.
We are insignificant and despised,
but we don't forget Your commandments.
Your justice is eternal,
and Your instructions are perfectly true.
As pressure and stress bear down on us,
we find joy in Your commands.
Your laws are always right;
Help us to understand them so we may live.

Your Word is good.

We pray with all our heart; Answer us, LORD!
We will obey Your decrees.
We cry out to You; Rescue us, that we may obey Your laws.
We rise early, before the sun is up;
    We cry out for help and put our hope in Your words.
We stay awake through the night,
    thinking about Your promise.
In Your faithful love, O LORD, hear our cry;
    Let us be revived by following Your regulations.
Lawless people are coming to attack us;
    They live far from Your instructions.
But You are near, O LORD, and all Your commands are true.
We have known from our earliest days
    that Your laws will last forever.

Look upon our suffering and rescue us,
    for we have not forgotten Your instructions.
Argue our case; Take our side!
Protect our lives as You promised.
The wicked are far from rescue,
    for they do not bother with Your decrees.
LORD, how great is Your mercy;
    Let us be revived by following Your regulations.
Many persecute and trouble us,
    yet we have not swerved from Your laws.
Seeing these traitors makes us sick at heart,
    because they care nothing for Your word.
See how we love Your commandments, LORD.
Give back our lives because of Your unfailing love.
The very essence of Your words is truth;
    All Your just regulations will stand forever.

Your Word is good.

Powerful people harass us without cause,
but our hearts tremble only at Your word.
We rejoice in Your word
like ones who discover a great treasure.
We hate and abhor all falsehood,
but we love Your instructions.
We will praise You seven times a day
because all Your regulations are just.
Those who love Your instructions have great peace
and do not stumble.
We long for Your rescue, LORD,
so we have obeyed Your commands.
We have obeyed Your laws, for we love them very much.
Yes, we obey Your commandments and laws
because You know everything we do.

O LORD, listen to our cry;
Give us the discerning minds You promised.
Listen to our prayer; Rescue us as You promised.
Let praise flow from our lips,
for You have taught us Your decrees.
Let our tongues sing about Your word,
for all Your commands are right.
Give us a helping hand,
for we have chosen to follow Your commandments.
O LORD, we have longed for Your rescue,
and Your instructions are our delight.
Let us live so we can praise You,
and may Your regulations help us.
We have wandered away like lost sheep;
Come and find us,
for we have not forgotten Your commands.

Your Word is good.

120

We bring our troubles to You, Lord.
We cry out to You, and You answer our prayer.
Rescue us, O Lord, from liars and from all deceitful people.
What will You do to those who deceive with their tongues?
Will You severely punish them?
You have told us that You will pierce them
with sharp arrows and burn them with glowing coals.

How we suffer, living in this broken world.
We are tired of living among people who hate peace.
We search for peace;
But when we speak of peace, they want war!

You answer our prayer.
You will punish the wicked.

121

We look up to the mountains;
From where does our help come?
Our help comes from You, LORD,
who made heaven and earth!

You will not let us stumble;
You, who watches over us, will not slumber.
Indeed, You, who watches over Israel,
never slumbers or sleeps.

You watch over us!
You stand beside us as our protective shade.
The sun will not harm us by day, nor the moon at night.

You keep us from all harm and watch over our lives.
You keep watch over us as we come and go,
both now and forever.

You made heaven and earth.
You will not let us stumble.
You watch over us.
You never sleep.
You stand beside us.
You keep us from all harm.
You keep watch over us.

122

The psalmist was glad when those around him said,
"Let me go to the house of the LORD."

While he was there, standing inside Jerusalem's gates,
he noted:

- that it was a well-built city,
  with seamless walls that could not be breached;
- that all the tribes of Israel—Your people—
  made their pilgrimage there,
  to give thanks to Your name,
  as the law required of them; and
- that in Jerusalem stood the thrones
  where judgment was given,
  the thrones of the dynasty of David.

We pray for peace in Jerusalem.
May all who love it prosper.

May there be peace within its walls
and prosperity in its palaces.

For the sake of our families and friends,
we will say, "May Jerusalem have peace."

For the sake of Your house, O LORD, our God,
we will seek what is best for Jerusalem.

You love Jerusalem.

123

We lift our eyes to You, O God, the One enthroned in heaven.
We keep looking to You, our God, for Your mercy,
  just as servants keep their eyes on their master,
  as a slave girl watches her mistress for the slightest signal.

Have mercy on us, LORD, have mercy,
  for we have had our fill of contempt.
We have had more than our fill of the scoffing of the proud
  and the contempt of the arrogant.

You are enthroned in heaven.
You give mercy.

124

What if You were not on our side?
What if You were not on our side when people attacked us?
They would have swallowed us alive in their burning anger.
The waters would have engulfed us;
  The current would have overwhelmed us.
Yes, the raging waters of their fury
  would have overwhelmed our very lives.

We praise You, LORD,
  who did not let their teeth tear us apart!
We escaped like birds from a hunter's trap.
The trap is broken, and we are free!
Our help is from You, LORD, who made heaven and earth.

You are on our side.
You made heaven and earth.

125

Those who trust in You, LORD, are as secure as Mount Zion;
They will not be defeated but will endure forever.
Just as the mountains surround Jerusalem,
so You surround Your people, both now and forever.
The wicked will not rule the land of the godly,
for then the godly might be tempted to do wrong.

O LORD, do good to those who are good,
whose hearts are in tune with You.
But banish those who turn to crooked ways, O LORD.
Take them away with those who do evil.
May Israel have peace!

You surround us.

126

When the Lord brought back his exiles to Jerusalem,
    it was like a dream.
They were filled with laughter, and they sang for joy.
And the other nations said,
    "What amazing things the Lord has done for them."
And You had done amazing things for them,
    and they were glad.
You have done amazing things for us, Lord, and we are glad!

Restore our well-being, Lord,
    as streams renew the desert.
You tell us that those who plant in tears
    will harvest with shouts of joy
    and that they who weep as they go to plant their seed
    will sing as they return with the harvest.

Restore our well-being, Lord.

You do amazing things for us.

127

Unless You build the house,
they work in vain who build it.
Unless You guard the city,
the watchman keeps awake in vain.
It is useless for us to work so hard,
from early morning until late at night,
anxiously working for food to eat;
For You give to us, Your beloved, even in our sleep.

Our children are a gift from You;
They are a reward from You.
Our children are like arrows in a warrior's hands.
We are so blessed to have a quiver full of them!
We will not be put to shame
when we confront our accusers at the city gates.

You are our provider.

128

How joyful are those who fear You, LORD—
all who follow Your ways!

You tell us that we will enjoy the fruit of our labor;
that we will be joyful and prosperous;
that the wives among us will be like fruitful grapevines,
flourishing within our homes;
that our children will be like vigorous young olive trees,
as they sit around our tables;
that this is Your blessing for those who fear You.

LORD, please continue to bless us.
May we see Jerusalem prosper as long as we live.
May we live to enjoy our grandchildren.
May Israel have peace!

You bless those who fear You.

129

From our earliest days our enemies have persecuted us,
but they have never defeated us.
Our backs are covered with cuts,
as if a farmer had plowed upon our backs.
But You are good, LORD;
You have cut us free from the ropes of the ungodly.

May all who hate Jerusalem
be turned back in shameful defeat.
May they be as useless as grass on a rooftop,
which withers before it grows up,
ignored by the harvester,
despised by the binder.

Though many who pass by
may refuse to give them this blessing:
"The LORD bless you; We bless you in the LORD's name;"
LORD, give us the courage and compassion
to ask You to bless our enemies with salvation.

You are good.

130

From the depths of despair, O LORD, we call for Your help.
Hear our cry, O Lord.
Pay attention to our prayer.
LORD, if You kept a record of our sins,
who, O Lord, could ever survive?
But You offer forgiveness, that we might learn to fear You.

We are counting on You, LORD;
Yes, we are counting on You.
We have put our hope in Your word.
We long for You more than sentries long for the dawn,
yes, more than sentries long for the dawn.

We hope in You, LORD; For with You there is unfailing love.
Your redemption overflows.
You will redeem Israel from every kind of sin.

You keep no record of our sins.
You offer forgiveness.
You love us with unfailing love.
Your redemption overflows.

131

LORD, our hearts are not proud; Our eyes are not haughty.
We don't concern ourselves with matters too great
  or too awesome for us to grasp.
Instead, we have calmed and quieted ourselves,
  like weaned children
  who no longer cry for their mothers' milk.

Yes, like weaned children are our souls within us.
We put our hope in You, LORD—now and always.

You are our hope.

132

LORD, remember David and all that he suffered.
He made a solemn promise to You.
He vowed to You, the Mighty One of Israel:

"I will not go home; I will not let myself rest.
I will not let my eyes sleep nor close my eyelids in slumber
until I find a place to build a house for the LORD,
a sanctuary for the Mighty One of Israel."

Israel heard that the Ark was in Ephrathah;
Then they found it in the distant countryside of Jaar.

As they went to Your dwelling place, LORD,
let us come before You;
Let us worship at the footstool of Your throne.

As they asked You to arise and enter Your resting place,
along with the Ark, the symbol of Your power,
and that Your priests would be clothed in godliness
and that Your loyal servants would sing for joy,
let us, likewise, be clothed in godliness and sing for joy.

For the sake of Your servant David,
do not reject Your chosen king.
You swore an oath to David
with a promise You will never take back:

"I will place one of your descendants on your throne.
If your descendants obey the terms of My covenant
and the laws that I teach them,
then your royal line will continue forever and ever."

You make eternal promises.

For You chose Jerusalem; You desired it for Your home.
You said:

"This is My resting place forever.
I will live here, for this is the home I desired.
I will bless this city and make it prosperous;
  I will satisfy its poor with food.
I will clothe its priests with godliness;
  Its faithful servants will sing for joy.
Here I will increase the power of David;
  My anointed one will be a light for My people.
I will clothe his enemies with shame,
  but he will be a glorious king."

You make eternal promises.

133

How wonderful and pleasant it is
for brothers live together in harmony!

For harmony is as precious as the anointing oil
that was poured over Aaron's head,
that ran down his beard and onto the border of his robe.

Harmony is as refreshing as the dew from Mount Hermon
that falls on the mountains of Zion.

And there You pronounced Your blessing, eternal life.

You give eternal life.

134

We praise You, Lord, as Your servants.

We lift up our hands to You and praise You.

Bless us, Lord, You who made heaven and earth.

You are praiseworthy.
You made heaven and earth.

135

We praise You, LORD!
We praise Your name!

We praise You, as Your servants,
like those who served in Your house,
in the courts of the Your house.

We praise You, LORD, for You are good;
We will celebrate Your lovely name with music.

You chose Jacob for Yourself,
Israel for Your own special treasure.
We know Your greatness, LORD—
that You are greater than any other god.
You do whatever You please,
throughout all heaven and earth,
and on the seas and in their depths.
You cause the clouds to rise over the whole earth.
You send the lightning with the rain
and release the wind from Your storehouses.
You destroyed the firstborn in each Egyptian home,
both people and animals.
You performed miraculous signs and wonders in Egypt
against Pharaoh and all his people.
You struck down great nations
and slaughtered mighty kings—
Sihon king of the Amorites,
Og king of Bashan, and all the kings of Canaan.

You are praiseworthy.
You are good.
You are greater than any other god.
You do whatever You please.

You gave their land as an inheritance,
a special possession to Your people Israel.
Your name, O Lord, endures forever;
Your fame, O Lord, is known to every generation.
For You will give justice to Your people
and have compassion on Your servants.

The idols of the nations are merely things of silver and gold,
shaped by human hands.
They have mouths but cannot speak, and eyes but cannot see.
They have ears but cannot hear,
and mouths but cannot breathe.
And those who make idols are just like them,
as are all who trust in them.

May Israel praise You, Lord!
May the priests—descendants of Aaron—praise You, Lord!
May the Levites, praise You, Lord!
May all who fear You, praise You, Lord!
May You, who lives in Jerusalem, be praised from Zion.

We praise You, Lord!

Your name endures forever.
You will give justice to Your people.
You will have compassion on Your servants.

136

We give thanks to You, LORD, for You are good!
Your faithful love endures forever.

We give thanks to You, the God of gods.
Your faithful love endures forever.

We give thanks to You, the Lord of lords.
Your faithful love endures forever.

We give thanks to You, who alone does mighty miracles.
Your faithful love endures forever.

We give thanks to You, who made the heavens so skillfully.
Your faithful love endures forever.

We give thanks to You, who placed the earth among the waters.
Your faithful love endures forever.

We give thanks to You, who made the heavenly lights—
Your faithful love endures forever.

the sun to rule the day,
Your faithful love endures forever.

and the moon and stars to rule the night.
Your faithful love endures forever.

We give thanks to You, who killed the firstborn of Egypt.
Your faithful love endures forever.

You are good.
You alone do mighty miracles.
You made the heavens.
Your faithful love endures forever.

You brought Israel out of Egypt.
Your faithful love endures forever.

You acted with a strong hand and powerful arm.
Your faithful love endures forever.

We give thanks to You, who parted the Red Sea.
Your faithful love endures forever.

You led Israel safely through,
Your faithful love endures forever.

but You hurled Pharaoh and his army into the Red Sea.
Your faithful love endures forever.

We give thanks to You,
who led Your people through the wilderness.
Your faithful love endures forever.

We give thanks to You, who struck down mighty kings.
Your faithful love endures forever.

You killed powerful kings—
Your faithful love endures forever.

Sihon, king of the Amorites,
Your faithful love endures forever.

and Og, king of Bashan.
Your faithful love endures forever.

You brought Israel out of Egypt.
Your faithful love endures forever.

You gave the land of these kings as an inheritance—
Your faithful love endures forever.

a special possession to Your servant Israel.
Your faithful love endures forever.

You remembered us in our weakness.
Your faithful love endures forever.

You saved us from our enemies.
Your faithful love endures forever.

You give food to every living thing.
Your faithful love endures forever.

We give thanks to You, the God of heaven.
Your faithful love endures forever.

You remembered us in our weakness.
You saved us from our enemies.
You give food to every living thing.
Your faithful love endures forever.

137

Your people sat and wept by the rivers of Babylon,
as they thought of Jerusalem.
They put away their harps,
hanging them on the branches of poplar trees.
For their captors demanded a song from them.
Their tormentors insisted on a joyful hymn, saying:
"Sing me one of those songs of Jerusalem!"

Your people said:

"How can we sing the songs of the LORD
while in a pagan land?
If we forget you, O Jerusalem,
let our right hands forget how to play the harp.
May our tongues stick to the roofs of our mouths
if we fail to remember you,
if we don't make Jerusalem our greatest joy.

O LORD, remember what the Edomites did
on the day the armies of Babylon captured Jerusalem.
'Destroy it!' they yelled. 'Level it to the ground!'

O Babylon, you will be destroyed.
Happy is the one who pays you back
for what you have done to us.
Happy is the one who takes your babies
and smashes them against the rocks!"

O LORD, may we not fail to remember You;
May You always be our greatest joy.

You will execute justice.

138

We give You thanks, O Lord, with all our heart;
We will sing Your praises before the gods.
We bow before Your holy temple as we worship.
We praise Your name, for Your unfailing love and faithfulness;
For Your promises are backed
by all the honor of Your name.
As soon as we pray, You answer us;
You encourage us by giving us strength.

Every king in all the earth will thank You, Lord,
for all of them will hear Your words.
Yes, they will sing about Your ways,
for Your glory is very great.
Though You are great, You care for the humble,
but You keep Your distance from the proud.

Your love is unfailing.
Your promises are backed by Your name.
You answer us.
You encourage us.
You give us strength.
Your glory is very great.
You are great.
You care for the humble.
You keep Your distance from the proud.

Though we are surrounded by troubles,
  You will protect us from the anger of our enemies.
You reach out Your hand,
  and the power of Your right hand saves us.
You will work out Your plans for our lives—
  for Your faithful love, O Lord, endures forever.
Don't abandon us, for You made us.

You will protect us.
You will work out Your plans for our lives.
Your love endures forever.
You made us.

139

O Lord, You have searched us and known us.
You know when we sit down and when we rise up;
You understand our thoughts from afar.
You scrutinize our paths and our lying down,
and are intimately acquainted with all our ways.

Even before there is a word on our tongues,
behold, O Lord, You know it all.
You have enclosed us behind and before,
and laid Your hand upon us.
Such knowledge is too wonderful for us;
It is too high, we cannot attain to it.

Where can we go from Your Spirit?
Or where can we flee from Your presence?
If we ascend to heaven, You are there;
If we make our beds in Sheol, behold, You are there.
If we take the wings of the dawn,
if we dwell in the remotest part of the sea,
even there Your hand will lead us,
and Your right hand will lay hold of us.

If we say, "Surely the darkness will overwhelm us,
and the light around us will be night,"
Even the darkness is not dark to You,
and the night is as bright as the day.
Darkness and light are alike to You.

You know us.
You understand our thoughts.
You are intimately acquainted with all our ways.
You know everything.
You are everywhere.

For You formed our inward parts;
You wove us in our mothers' wombs.
We will give thanks to You,
for we are fearfully and wonderfully made.
Wonderful are Your works, and our souls know it very well.

Our frames were not hidden from You
when we were made in secret
and skillfully wrought in the depths of the earth.
Your eyes have seen our unformed substance;
And in Your book were all written
the days that were ordained for us,
when as yet there was not one of them.

How precious also are Your thoughts to us, O God!
How vast is the sum of them!
If we should count them, they would outnumber the sand.

When we awake, we are still with You.
At times we want You to slay the wicked, O God,
and to make the men of bloodshed depart from us;
For they speak against You wickedly,
and Your enemies take Your name in vain.

Should we not hate those who hate You, O Lord?
And should we not loathe those who rise up against You?
At times, we hate them with the utmost hatred;
They have become our enemies.
But You tell us to love them and pray for them.
Search us, O God, and know our hearts;
Try us and know our anxious thoughts;
And see if there be any hurtful way in us,
and lead us in the everlasting way.

You created us with great care.
You control everything.

140

O Lord, rescue us from evil people.
Protect us from those who are violent,
those who plot evil in their hearts
and stir up trouble all day long.
Their tongues sting like a snake;
the venom of a viper drips from their lips.

O Lord, keep us out of the hands of the wicked.
Protect us from those who are violent,
for they are plotting against us.
The proud have set a trap to catch us;
They have stretched out a net;
They have placed traps all along the way.

You are our God!
Listen, O Lord, to our cries for mercy!
O Sovereign Lord, the strong one who rescues us,
You protect us in the day of battle.
Lord, do not let evil people have their way.
Do not let their evil schemes succeed,
or they will become proud.

Lord, we want to say:

"Let our enemies be destroyed
by the very evil they have planned for us.
Let burning coals fall down on their heads.
Let them be thrown into the fire
or into watery pits from which they can't escape.
Don't let liars prosper here in our land.
Cause great disasters to fall on the violent."

You are our God.

But You tell us to love our enemies
  and to pray for those who persecute us;
  And we trust You.
For we know You will help those they persecute;
  You will give justice to the poor.
Surely righteous people are praising Your name;
  And the godly will live in Your presence.

You protect us.
You give justice to the poor.

141

O Lord, we are calling to You. Please hurry!
   Listen when we cry to You for help!
Accept our prayer as incense offered to You,
   and our upraised hands as an evening offering.

Take control of what we say, O Lord,
   and guard our lips.
Don't let us drift toward evil
   or take part in acts of wickedness.
Don't let us share in the delicacies
   of those who do wrong.

Let the godly strike us;
   It will be a kindness.
If they correct us, it is soothing medicine;
   Don't let us refuse it.

But we pray constantly
   against the wicked and their deeds.
When their leaders are thrown down from a cliff,
   the wicked will listen to our words and find them true.
Like rocks brought up by a plow,
   the bones of the wicked will lie scattered without burial.

We look to You for help, O Sovereign Lord.
You are our refuge; Don't let them kill us.
Keep us from the traps they have set for us,
   from the snares of those who do wrong.
Let the wicked fall into their own nets,
   but let us escape.

You are our refuge.

142

We cry out to You, LORD;
  We plead for Your mercy.
We pour out our complaints before You
  and tell You all our troubles.
When we are overwhelmed,
  You alone know the way we should turn.
Wherever we go,
  our enemies have set traps for us.

We look for someone to come and help us,
  but it seems like no one gives us a passing thought,
  like no one will help us,
  like no one cares a bit what happens to us.

So we cry out to You, O LORD.
We say:

  "You are our place of refuge.
  You are all we really want in life.
  Hear our cry, for we are very low.
  Rescue us from our persecutors,
    for they are too strong for us.
  Bring our souls out of prison so we can thank You.
  The godly will surround us, for You are good to us."

You alone know our paths.
You are our place of refuge.
You are good to us.

143

Hear our prayer, O LORD; Listen to our plea!
Answer us because You are faithful and righteous.
Don't put Your servants on trial,
  for no one is innocent before You.
Our enemy has chased us.
He has knocked us to the ground
  and forces us to live in darkness like those in the grave.
We are losing all hope; We are paralyzed with fear.
We remember the days of old.
We ponder all Your great works
  and think about what You have done.
We lift our hands to You in prayer.
We thirst for You as parched land thirsts for rain.

Come quickly, LORD, and answer us,
  for our depression deepens.
Don't turn away from us, or we will die.
Let us hear of Your unfailing love each morning,
  for we are trusting You.
Show us where to walk, for we give ourselves to You.
Rescue us from our enemies, LORD;
  We run to You to hide us.
Teach us to do Your will, for You are our God.
May Your gracious Spirit lead us forward
  on a firm footing.
For the glory of Your name, O LORD, preserve our lives.
Because of Your faithfulness, bring us out of this distress.
In Your unfailing love, silence all our enemies
  and subdue all our foes, for we are Your servants.

You are faithful and righteous.
Your love is unfailing.
You are our God.
Your Spirit leads us.

144

We praise You, LORD, our rock.
You train our hands for war
  and give our fingers skill for battle.
You are our loving ally and our fortress,
  our tower of safety, our rescuer.
You are our shield, and we take refuge in You.
You subdue people under us.

O LORD, what are human beings that You should notice them,
  mere mortals that You should think about them?
For they are like a breath of air;
  Their days are like a passing shadow.
Open the heavens, LORD, and come down.
Touch the mountains so they billow smoke.
Hurl Your lightning bolts and scatter Your enemies!
Shoot Your arrows and confuse them!
Reach down from heaven and rescue us;
  Rescue us from deep waters,
  from the power of our enemies.

Their mouths are full of lies;
  They swear to tell the truth, but they lie instead.
We will sing a new song to You, O God!
We will sing Your praises.
For You grant victory to kings!
You rescued Your servant David from the fatal sword.
Save us and rescue us from the power of our enemies.
Their mouths are full of lies;
  They swear to tell the truth, but they lie instead.

You are our ally, our fortress, and our tower of safety.
You are our rescuer, our shield, and our refuge.

As David asked that Israel's sons
would flourish in their youth,
like well-nurtured plants;
that their daughters would be like graceful pillars,
carved to beautify a palace;
that their barns would be filled with crops of every kind;
that the flocks in their fields
would multiply by the thousands,
even tens of thousands;
that their oxen would be loaded down with produce; and
that there would be no enemy breaking through their walls,
no going into captivity, and
no cries of alarm in their town squares,
LORD, please provide for us in such ways.

Yes, joyful are those who live like this!
Joyful indeed are those who make You their God.

You give joy.

145

We will exalt You, our God and King,
  and praise Your name forever and ever.
We will praise You every day;
  Yes, we will praise You forever.
Great are You, LORD! You are most worthy of praise!
No one can measure Your greatness.

Let each generation tell its children of Your mighty acts;
  Let them proclaim Your power.
We will meditate on Your majestic, glorious splendor
  and Your wonderful miracles.
Your awe-inspiring deeds will be on every tongue;
  We will proclaim Your greatness.
Everyone will share the story of Your wonderful goodness;
  They will sing with joy about Your righteousness.

You are merciful and compassionate,
  slow to get angry and filled with unfailing love.
You are good to everyone.
You shower compassion on all Your creation.
All of Your works will thank You, LORD,
  and Your faithful followers will praise You.
They will speak of the glory of Your kingdom;
  They will give examples of Your power.
They will tell about Your mighty deeds
  and about the majesty and glory of Your reign.

You are great.
You are most worthy of praise.
You are merciful and compassionate.
You are slow to get angry.
You are filled with unfailing love.
You are good to everyone.
You shower compassion on all Your creation.

For Your kingdom is an everlasting kingdom.
You rule throughout all generations.
You always keep Your promises;
  You are gracious in all You do.
You help the fallen and lift those bent beneath their loads.

The eyes of all look to You in hope;
  You give them their food as they need it.
When You open Your hand,
  You satisfy the hunger and thirst of every living thing.
You are righteous in everything You do;
  You are filled with kindness.
You are close to all who call on You,
  yes, to all who call on You in truth.
You grant the desires of those who fear You;
  You hear their cries for help and rescue them.
You protect all those who love You,
  but You destroy the wicked.

We praise You, LORD, and may everyone on earth
  bless Your holy name forever and ever.

Your kingdom is an everlasting kingdom.
You rule throughout all generations.
You always keep Your promises.
You are gracious in all You do.
You help the fallen.
You satisfy the hunger and thirst of every living thing.
You are righteous in everything You do.
You are filled with kindness.
You are close to all who call on You in truth.
You hear the cries for help those who fear You.
You grant the desires of those who fear You.
You rescue those who fear You.
You protect those who love You.
You destroy the wicked.

146

We praise You, LORD!

Let all that we are praise You.
We will praise You as long as we live.
We will sing praises to You, our God, with our dying breath.
We will not put our confidence in powerful people;
  There is no help for us there.
When they breathe their last, they return to the earth,
  and all their plans die with them.

But we are joyful because we have You,
  the God of Israel, as our helper.
Our hope is in You, our God.

You made heaven and earth,
  the sea, and everything in them.
You keep every promise forever.
You give justice to the oppressed
  and food to the hungry.
You free the prisoners.
You open the eyes of the blind.

You are our hope.
You made heaven and earth.
You keep every promise forever.
You give justice to the oppressed.
You give food to the hungry.
You free the prisoners.
You open the eyes of the blind.

You lift up those who are weighed down.
You love the godly.
You protect the foreigners around us.
You care for the orphans and widows,
but You frustrate the plans of the wicked.

You will reign forever.
You will be our God.

We praise You, LORD!

You lift up those who are weighed down.
You love the godly.
You protect the foreigners around us.
You care for orphans and widows.
You frustrate the plans of the wicked.
You will reign forever.
You are our God.

147

We praise You, LORD!

How good to sing praises to You, our God!
How delightful and how fitting!
You are rebuilding Jerusalem
    and bringing the exiles back to Israel.
You heal the brokenhearted and bandage their wounds.
You count the stars and call them all by name.

How great are You, Lord! Your power is absolute!
Your understanding is beyond comprehension!
You support the humble,
    but You bring the wicked down into the dust.
We sing out our thanks to You, LORD;
    We sing praises to You, our God.

You cover the heavens with clouds, provide rain for the earth,
    and make the grass grow in mountain pastures.
You give food to the wild animals
    and feed the young ravens when they cry.
You take no pleasure in the strength of a horse
    or in human might.
No, Your delight is in those who fear You,
    those who put their hope in Your unfailing love.
We will glorify You, LORD.
We will praise You, our God.

You heal the brokenhearted.
Your power is absolute.
Your understanding is beyond comprehension.
You support the humble.
You bring the wicked down into the dust.
You provide for the earth.
You delight in those who fear You.

For You have strengthened the bars of our gates
    and blessed the children within our walls.
You send peace across our nation
    and satisfy our hunger with the finest wheat.
You send Your orders to the world—
    how swiftly Your word flies!
You send the snow like white wool;
    You scatter frost upon the ground like ashes.
You hurl the hail like stones.
Who can stand against Your freezing cold?
Then, at Your command, it all melts.
You send Your winds, and the ice thaws.

You have revealed Your words to Jacob,
    Your decrees and regulations to Israel.
You have not done this for any other nation;
    They do not know Your regulations.

We praise You LORD!

Your love is unfailing.
You send peace.
You satisfy our hunger.

148

We praise You, Lord!

May the heavens praise You.
May the skies praise You.
May all angels praise You.
May all the armies of heaven praise You.
May the sun and moon praise You.
May all twinkling stars praise You.
May the skies above praise You.
May the vapors high above the clouds praise You.
May every created thing give praise to You, Lord,
for You issued Your command, and they came into being.

You established them forever and ever.
Your decree will never be revoked.

May the creatures of the ocean depths
praise You from the earth.

Fire and hail, snow and clouds,
wind and weather that obey You,
mountains and all hills,
fruit trees and all cedars,
wild animals and all livestock,
small scurrying animals and birds,
kings of the earth and all people,
rulers and judges of the earth,
young men and young women,
old men and children;
May they all praise Your name.

You created everything.

For Your name is very great;
  Your glory towers over the earth and heaven!

You have made Your people strong,
  honoring Your faithful ones—
  the people of Israel who are close to You.

We praise You, LORD!

Your name is very great.
You made us strong.

149

We praise You, LORD!

We will sing a new song to You.
We will sing Your praises in the assembly of the faithful.
We will rejoice in You, our Maker.
We will exult in You, our King.
We will praise Your name with dancing and music.

For You delight in Your people;
  You crown the humble with victory.
We will rejoice that You honor us.
We will sing for joy as we lie on our beds.

Your praises will be in our mouths,
  as it was with Your people long ago,
  who held a sharp sword in their hands—
  to execute vengeance on the nations
  and punishment on the peoples,
  to bind their kings with shackles
  and their leaders with iron chains,
  to execute the judgment written against them.

Such vindication is an honor for Your faithful ones.

We praise You, LORD!

You delight in Your people.
You crown the humble with victory.

150

We praise You, LORD!

We praise You in Your sanctuary.
We praise You in Your mighty heaven.
We praise You for Your mighty works.
We praise Your unequaled greatness.
We praise You with a blast of the ram's horn.
We praise You with the lyre and harp.
We praise You with the tambourine and dancing.
We praise You with strings and flutes.
We praise You with a clash of cymbals.
We praise You with loud clanging cymbals.

May everything that breathes sing praises to You, LORD!

We praise You, LORD!

Your greatness is unequaled.

You guard our way. You are mighty. You are sovereign. You are our refuge. You are a shield around us. You are our glory. You are the lifter of our heads. You answer us when we cry out to You. You watch over us. You save us. You are our liberator. You hear us when we call. You give us joy. You are our protector. You take no pleasure in wickedness. You bless the godly. You answer our prayers. You judge the nations. You are our shield. You are just. You are majestic. You created everything. You reign forever. You care for the helpless. You are a shelter for the oppressed. You are just. You are alive. You see everything. You defend the orphans and the oppressed. You are King forever and ever. You rule from heaven. You are righteous. Your promises are pure. You will protect the oppressed. You love us. You saved us. You are good to us. You are with us. You are our protector. You are holy. You are our Lord. You are our inheritance. You are our ultimate joy. You see those who do right. You are our protector. You are our rock. You are our fortress. You are our savior. You are our shield. You are the power that saves us. You are our place of safety. You are worthy of praise. You have rescued us. You have rewarded us. Your way is perfect. Your promises prove true. You live. Your love is unfailing. You are the mighty Creator. Your law is perfect. Your testimony is sure. Your precepts are right. Your commandment is pure. Your laws are true. Your laws are sweeter than honey. Your laws are a warning. Your laws are a reward. You are our rock. You are our redeemer. You answer our prayers. Your name alone is powerful. You are all powerful. You are holy. You listen to the cries of the needy. You rule all the nations. You are our shepherd. You are with us. You are our inheritance. You are invincible in battle. You are the King of Glory. You are merciful. You are good. You do what is right. You are our friend. You rescue us. You are our hope. You are faithful. You are our light. You are our salvation. You are our fortress. You will never abandon us. You are just. You hear us. You are our strength. You help us. You fill our hearts with joy. You are majestic. You are the Eternal King. You heal us. You turn our sorrow to joy. You are our refuge. You are our hope. You are our hiding place. You are our guide. You are Creator of all. You are our hope. You are our help. You are our shield. You are great. You answer us. You free us from all our fears. You rescue us from all our troubles. You are near to us when we are brokenhearted. You vindicate us. You are just. You are the fountain of life. Your love never fails. You give us the desires of our hearts. You will destroy the wicked. You take care of the godly. You take care of the innocent. You direct the steps of the godly. You delight in every detail of our lives. You hold us by the hand. You love justice. You will never abandon us. You will keep us safe forever. You will not let the wicked succeed. You will not let us be condemned. You will honor us. You will destroy the rebellious. You will rescue us. You are our fortress. You help us. You rescue us from the wicked. You save us. You are our shelter. You hear our every sigh. You are our Savior. You are our only hope. You discipline us. You turn to us. You hear our cries. You lift us out of despair. You give us a new song to sing. You have no equal. You take no delight in sacrifices. You are faithful. Your love is unfailing. You are great. You are our helper and our savior. You care for the poor. You are the Great Healer. You give us access to Your presence. You are worthy of all praise. You are alive. You are the Living Water. You are our Savior. You are our God. You give us life. You are our rock. You have not forgotten us. You are our Savior. You are our God. You are our only safe haven. You are the source of all our joy. You are our Savior. You are our God. You give us victory. You know the secrets of every heart. You are our King and our God. You are our Redeemer. You are the most handsome of all. You are a warrior.

You defend truth, humility, and justice. You love justice and hate evil. You will exalt us. You are worthy of all honor and praise forever and ever. You are our refuge and strength. You are here with us. You are our fortress. You are God. You will be exalted among the nations. You will be exalted in the earth. You are awesome. You rule the whole earth. You are great. You deserve all praise. Your love is unfailing. You are our God forever and ever. You are our guide. You are our Redeemer. You have power over the grave. You shine in glorious radiance. You will not remain silent. You need nothing. You will rescue us and honor us. You are justified when You speak. You are blameless when You judge. You will make us know wisdom. You do not delight in sacrifice. You are not pleased with burnt offering. You delight in a broken spirit and a contrite heart. Your justice continues forever. Your love is unfailing. You will scatter the bones of Your enemies. You brought salvation out of Jerusalem. You are our helper. You keep us alive. Your name is good. You have rescued us. You will rescue us. You hear our voices. You ransom us and keep us safe. You have ruled forever. You will take care of us. You will not permit the godly to slip and fall. You will save us. You are for us. You keep Your promises. You have delivered our souls from death. You keep our feet from stumbling. You are worthy of all our trust. You will save us from our enemies. You are worthy of all praise. You will judge the earth. You will bring justice. You scoff at all the hostile nations. You are our strength, our fortress, and our refuge. You will rescue us. You will stand with us. You are our strength. You show us unfailing love. You will lead us. You will never reject us. You will enable us to do mighty things. You are our rock. You are our safe refuge. You are a fortress, protecting us from our enemies. You have given us an inheritance of eternity with You. You alone are our rock and our salvation. You are our fortress. You are our refuge. You repay all people according to what they have done. You are our God. Your unfailing love is better than life itself. You hold us securely. You hear our complaints. You will bring justice. You protect us. You answer our prayers. You forgive our sins. You are our savior. You are the hope of everyone on earth. You formed the mountains by Your power. You inspire shouts of joy. You take care of the earth. Your deeds are awesome. You keep our feet from stumbling. You have purified us like silver. You pay attention to our prayers. You love us perpetually. You govern the nations with justice. You bless us. Your name is the LORD. You set the prisoners free. You are our Savior. You carry us in Your arms. You rescue us from death. You are the source of life. You give power and strength to Your people. You know us. You give us faith. Your love is unfailing. Your salvation is sure. Your unfailing love is wonderful. Your mercy is plentiful. You are our rescuer. You hear the cries of the needy. You are our helper. You are our savior. You do what is right. You are our rock and our fortress. You alone are our hope. You have cared for us from birth. You alone are just. You will restore us. You are faithful to Your promises. You have ransomed us. Your Son will rule all. You defend the poor. You rescue the children of the needy. You crush the oppressor. Your name will endure forever. You will judge the wicked. You are our guide. You are our hearts' desire. You are our refuge. Your name is great. You are resplendent. You judge those who do evil. You are to be feared. You break the spirit of rulers. Your ways are holy. You are the God of great wonders. You redeem Your people. You've done great and miraculous things throughout history. You are patient, not wanting any to perish but for all to come to repentance. You lead Your people. You are enthroned above the cherubim. You are the God of heaven's armies. You are our only means of salvation. You are our strength. You are the giver of good things. You rule over everything.

You care for the poor and the orphan. You avenge Your people. You alone are the Lord *Most High. You are the living God. You are our King and our God. You are our sun and shield. You give us grace and glory. You give us good things. You speak peace to us. You pour down Your blessings on us. You are our God. You are so good. You are so ready to forgive. You are great and perform wonderful deeds. You alone are God. Your love for us is very great. You have rescued us. You are a God of compassion and mercy. You are slow to get angry. You are filled with unfailing love and faithfulness. You love Jerusalem. You are the source of all joy. You are the God of our salvation. Your unfailing love will last forever. You are entirely faithful. You created everything. You make us strong. You protect us. You cannot lie. You promise Your unfailing love. You are God. You see all our secret sins. Your love is unfailing. You alone are our refuge, our place of safety. You hear us when we call. You are our salvation. Your love is unfailing. You are forever faithful. You do great works. You are just. You are our rock. You are King. You are robed in majesty. You are eternal. You are mightier than the violent raging of the seas. You are mightier than the breakers on the shore. You are holy. You know people's thoughts. You will not abandon Your people. You are our fortress. You are the mighty rock. You will destroy evil people. You are a great God. You are a great King, above all gods. You made the sea and the dry land. You made us and watch over us. You speak to us. You welcome us into Your place of rest. You save. You are great. You are worthy of praise. You are to be feared. You made the heavens. You deserve all glory. You reign. You will judge everyone fairly. You are coming to judge the earth. You reign. You are supreme over all the earth. You protect the lives of Your faithful followers. You have done wonderful things. You have made known Your salvation. You have revealed Your righteousness to every nation. You are coming to judge the world with justice and fairness. You are our king. Your name is holy. You are holy. You are God. You made us. You are good. Your love and Your faithfulness endure forever. You deserve our praise and our full devotion. You will sit on Your throne forever. You will appear in Your glory. You live forever. You laid the foundation of the earth. You forgive all our sins. You fill our lives with good things. You are compassionate and gracious. You are slow to anger. You remove our transgressions from us. You rule over everything. You are great. You created everything. You maintain everything. You take pleasure in all You have made. You are great. You stand by Your covenant. You orchestrate everything. You brought Your people out of Egypt. You satisfied their hunger. You are good. You are so patient. You get angry when we turn from you. Your love is unfailing. You are good. You satisfy the thirsty soul. You are so powerful. Your love is great. You have done wonderful things. You rescue the poor from trouble. Your lovingkindness is great above the heavens. Your truth reaches to the skies. You will trample down our adversaries. You are worthy of praise. You are so faithful and good. You stand beside the needy. You stand ready to save. You give dominion to the King. Your deeds are amazing. Your righteousness never fails. You give food to those who fear You. You always remember Your covenant. You have paid our ransom in full. Your name is holy and awe-inspiring. You bless those who fear You and walk in Your way. You are high above the nations. Your glory is higher than the heavens. You are beyond comparison. You are enthroned on high. You care for the poor. Your presence causes the whole earth to tremble. You are worthy of all glory. You are our help and our shield. You will bless us. You hear us. You are kind. You are good. You are merciful. You protect those of childlike faith. You have been good to us. You have saved us from death. You have freed us from our chains.*

Your unfailing love for us is powerful. Your faithfulness endures forever. You are good. Your love endures forever. You answer us and set us free. You are for us, and You will help us. You are our strength and our song. You give us victory. You are the creator of each day. You are our God. You are good. Your love endures forever. Your Word is good. You answer our prayer. You will punish the wicked. You made heaven and earth. You will not let us stumble. You watch over us. You never sleep. You stand beside us. You keep us from all harm. You keep watch over us. You love Jerusalem. You are enthroned in heaven. You give mercy. You are on our side. You made heaven and earth. You surround us. You do amazing things for us. You are our provider. You bless those who fear You. You are good. You keep no record of our sins. You offer forgiveness. You love us with unfailing love. Your redemption overflows. You are our hope. You make eternal promises. You give eternal life. You are praiseworthy. You made heaven and earth. You are praiseworthy. You are good. You are greater than any other god. You do whatever You please. Your name endures forever. You will give justice to Your people. You will have compassion on Your servants. You are good. You alone do mighty miracles. You made the heavens. You brought Israel out of Egypt. Your faithful love endures forever. You remembered us in our weakness. You saved us from our enemies. You give food to every living thing. Your faithful love endures forever. You will execute justice. Your love is unfailing. Your promises are backed by Your name. You answer us. You encourage us. You give us strength. Your glory is very great. You are great. You care for the humble. You keep Your distance from the proud. You will protect us. You will work out Your plans for our lives. Your love endures forever. You made us. You know us. You understand our thoughts. You are intimately acquainted with all our ways. You know everything. You are everywhere. You created us with great care. You control everything. You are our God. You protect us. You give justice to the poor. You are our refuge. You alone know our paths. You are our place of refuge. You are good to us. You are faithful and righteous. Your love is unfailing. You are our God. Your Spirit leads us. You are our ally, our fortress, and our tower of safety. You are our rescuer, our shield, and our refuge. You give joy. You are great. You are most worthy of praise. You are merciful and compassionate. You are slow to get angry. You are filled with unfailing love. You are good to everyone. You shower compassion on all Your creation. Your kingdom is an everlasting kingdom. You rule throughout all generations. You always keep Your promises. You are gracious in all You do. You help the fallen. You satisfy the hunger and thirst of every living thing. You are righteous in everything You do. You are filled with kindness. You are close to all who call on You in truth. You hear the cries for help those who fear You. You grant the desires of those who fear You. You rescue those who fear You. You protect those who love You. You destroy the wicked. You are our hope. You made heaven and earth. You keep every promise forever. You give justice to the oppressed. You give food to the hungry. You free the prisoners. You open the eyes of the blind. You lift up those who are weighed down. You love the godly. You protect the foreigners around us. You care for orphans and widows. You frustrate the plans of the wicked. You will reign forever. You are our God. You heal the brokenhearted. Your power is absolute. Your understanding is beyond comprehension. You support the humble. You bring the wicked down into the dust. You provide for the earth. You delight in those who fear You. Your love is unfailing. You send peace. You satisfy our hunger. You created everything. Your name is very great. Your name is very great. You delight in Your people. You crown the humble with victory. Your greatness is unequaled.